PREACHING BIBLICAL TEXTS

Preaching Biblical Texts

*Expositions by
Jewish and Christian Scholars*

Edited by

Fredrick C. Holmgren
and
Herman E. Schaalman

WILLIAM B. EERDMANS PUBLISHING COMPANY
GRAND RAPIDS, MICHIGAN

© 1995 Wm. B. Eerdmans Publishing Co.
255 Jefferson Ave. S.E., Grand Rapids, Michigan 49503

Printed in the United States of America

00 99 98 97 96 95   7 6 5 4 3 2 1

Library of Congress Cataloging-in-Publication Data

Preaching biblical texts: expositions by Jewish and Christian scholars /
edited by Fredrick C. Holmgren and Herman E. Schaalman.
    p.   cm.
Includes bibliographical references (p.).
ISBN 0-8028-0814-X (paper)
1. Bible. O.T. Pentateuch — Criticism, interpretation, etc.
2. Bible. O.T. Pentateuch — Criticism, interpretation, etc., Jewish. 3. Bible.
O.T. Pentateuch — Homiletical use.   I. Holmgren, Fredrick Carlson, 1926-   .
II. Schaalman, Herman E. (Herman Ezra), 1916-   .
BS1225.P73   1995
222'.106 — dc20   95-11804
                                CIP

Contents

Foreword

ELIE WIESEL

The sacred texts of the Bible were given to the people of Israel, who shared them with other nations. These texts should be read with fervor and passion. In reality, "read" is not the right word. We do not "read" the Book of Books; we study it. We penetrate more deeply into it as we celebrate it. We probe its hidden meaning in order to be brought back to Sinai. There the voice of God continues to resound, in the heart and memory of a threatened humanity that wavers between good and evil, indifference and compassion, life and death.

Since my childhood, without ever losing interest, I have continued to study the biblical stories that remain the foundation of Jewish history. Each reading brings with it a new excitement and previously unsuspected meaning.

Adam and Eve, Cain and Abel, Noah and his survival, Abraham and Isaac, Joseph and his brothers, Moses and the tragedy of his destiny: for decades I have tried to understand them, knowing all the while that I will never succeed.

To be sure, I know the broad outlines and certain details of their "biographies." Adam and Eve, as unfortunate parents, learn that their two sons are each other's assassin and victim. Where do they find the courage to begin all over again? Somehow they rise above their anguish and give birth to a third son, Seth. How can we explain their faith in the future?

And Noah: how can we explain his passivity when faced with the Lord's harsh, relentless will? God commands him to build a life-saving ark for himself and his family, and Noah obeys. Why doesn't he intercede for the innocent children of other families?

Abraham will do that, when he tries to save Sodom — but he fails utterly to plead with God to spare his own beloved son Isaac! The interrupted sacrifice of Isaac, a baffling but fascinating episode, and tragic from several points of view, has haunted more than one generation of martyrs. All the characters in this dream leave us perplexed. I do not understand God, who requires the sacrifice, or Abraham, who agrees to it. And why does Isaac submit to a divine order he did not receive himself?

Shall I continue this quest, which can only lead to more of the searching and questioning intrinsic to the history and psychology of the Jewish people?

Why is Jacob so timid in the presence of his brother Esau, and with Laban? Why does he leave it to the women to influence his decisions?

And Joseph, Jacob's cherished, coddled son — how could he live so many years as an all-powerful near sovereign in Egypt without sending emissaries to the land of Canaan to see if his father was still alive?

As for Joseph's brothers, the Talmud apparently criticizes them justly. Too egotistical, all of them. They throw their younger brother into a snake pit, and then dig into a presumably sumptuous meal. How can they eat, with their brother shrieking from pain and fright?

And Moses, prince of prophets, the immortal master of his people thirty for knowledge, God's messenger to Israel and the mouthpiece of Israel before God — how shall we interpret the punishments, sufferings, and humiliations he undergoes right up to the end of his life?

Before he dies, Moses hears God explain the reasons why he will die in the desert instead of leading his people to the Promised Land. God takes him to task for having failed in his mission, for his mistakes and transgressions — in short, for having betrayed him. How should we interpret such harshness and severity on God's part toward his chosen servant and prophet?

Today, I am far from the child I was, but that child's questions remain open questions — my questions. I learn these texts again, I study the midrashic commentaries on them: their mysterious light fascinates but does not soothe me. What next? I will carry on.

That is what the writers of this book do: they carry on, each in his own way, in his own style, with his own approach.

Does a Christian interpretation of the Bible exist? I have no idea. Christian scholars will have to answer that question. As a Jew, I can only emphasize the universal significance of this Jewish tradition. God chose to create Adam and Eve, who were not Jewish, as his way of saying to all men, to all women, from the beginning to the end of time, that they are all descendants of the same couple. No one should declare himself superior or inferior to others.

I have said elsewhere, but allow me to repeat, that when the Messiah comes, the people of earth will not all become Jews, but they will become more human.

Translated by JOYCE MAIN HANKS

Foreword

JOSEPH CARDINAL BERNARDIN

The book of Isaiah invites world-weary travelers on the journey of faith to draw near to the wisdom of God:

> All you who are thirsty, come to the water! You who have no money, come, receive grain and eat. Come, without paying and without cost. Drink wine and milk! Why spend your money for what is not bread, your wages for what fails to satisfy? Heed me, and you shall eat well. You shall delight in rich fare. Come to me heedfully, listen, that you may have life. (Isa. 55:1-3*a*)

The only condition for accepting God's gracious invitation is apparently a hunger and thirst for God. In return, believers receive life in all its fullness! Who could refuse such an invitation?

But how do we respond to this invitation, as believers, as preachers of the word of God? There are several ways, of course. On one level, carefully reading a biblical text is similar to listening attentively to a good friend. It requires that we set aside personal agendas, listen with our heart as well as our mind, be as open-minded as possible, and be willing to be surprised! The essays in this book reflect such careful, patient listening to biblical texts that have acquired considerable familiarity yet reveal new insights or levels of meaning to those who approach the texts with great attentiveness, faith, and reverence.

As believers, we rely daily on the nourishment and guidance of the Scriptures. We turn to them in times of joy and sorrow, in moments of success and failure, in seasons of hope and near despair. They provide us with comfort and consolation, insight and understanding, challenge and demands on the way we live. They reveal the divine plan of salvation and lead us deeper into the mystery of God.

As pastors, we turn to the Scriptures for wisdom and strength as we minister to the blind, the deaf, and the lame; as we reach out a helping hand to the poor, the hungry, and the homeless; as we seek justice for the widow, the orphan, and the immigrant; as we seek liberty for the oppressed, the persecuted, and the captives of substance abuse; as we challenge the self-sufficient, the powerful, and the apathetic; as we seek to enlighten the confused, bring God's forgiveness to the sinner, include the outcast and the alienated in the community of faith, and comfort the dying.

Yes, for Jews and Christians the word of God is an indispensable source of nourishment and guidance. It is also a *living* word. The Second Vatican Council acknowledged that our understanding of the word of God develops through the ages and that each generation must strive to understand and apply the biblical message in its own time — through contemplation and personal study, through an inner understanding that comes from spiritual experience, and from preaching within the community of faith.

Nevertheless, the Scriptures are ancient documents with a complex history of development and millennia of interpretations. That is why we also need scholars, according to the model of the scribe described by Ben Sira (Sirach 38:24 — 39:11), who can help us understand more clearly the living word of God addressed to us today in the ancient texts of the Scriptures. For Ben Sira, the scribe's main task was to study the law, prophets, and writings and to instruct others in this religious heritage and wisdom. This was not only an academic responsibility; it necessarily went hand in hand with "fear of the Lord," devotion to the word of God, and prayer.

Through the centuries, this scribal role has evolved with the changing circumstances and the ongoing development of the religious tradition. Today, biblical scholars and learned preachers play a similar role in communities of believers. These contemporary "scribes" are like the wise teacher of St. Matthew's Gospel (13:52) who is able to bring forth the old with the new — who has a great respect and esteem for and familiarity with the traditional texts and is able to discern and articulate their significance and relevance for contemporary life.

God has given the authors of the essays in this volume this marvelous ability. These Jewish and Christian scholars and preachers are firmly grounded in their respective religious tradition. They are familiar with the interpretation of the biblical text in their tradition through the centuries. They have also acquired expertise in modern biblical interpretive methods as well as a keen sensitivity to the particular circumstances of life in the contemporary world. In their study of several passages of the Torah or Pentateuch, they uncover various layers of meaning and articulate how their interpretation helps illuminate the human condition today in the light of the word of God.

I applaud this interfaith effort and hope that it is only the beginning of a series of such endeavors that will help preachers in our respective synagogues and churches to reflect and preach upon the Scriptures — and thereby be effective instruments through which God nourishes, guides, and challenges God's people.

Editors' Introduction

The source of life for the community of faith is the Word of God recorded in Scripture. This Word slips through the boundaries of time, as well as those of geography and culture, to address all whose ears are ready to hear. It is this "present" character of Scripture that underlies the expositions published in this volume. They focus on fourteen important passages from the Old Testament/Hebrew Bible and have in mind, primarily, pastors, rabbis, and priests who regularly interpret the Scriptures for their congregations.

Well-known Jewish and Christian scholars have cooperated in producing this volume, which concentrates on texts from the Torah/Pentateuch. In addition to providing a rich resource for preaching, this volume provides an opportunity for Christian and Jewish readers to become acquainted with the way in which the "other" tradition approaches and understands Scripture — and to discover that there are riches to be found outside the borders of one's own community.

These expositions are founded on solid scholarship, but they are not technical studies addressed to the scholarly community. Rather, they are focused interpretations that probe the "center" of the text in order to spark thought for and provide helpful guidance in the preparation of a sermon, homily, or biblical study. Although this volume speaks, at first level, to those in professional ministry, its content and style will appeal to lay leaders who desire a better understanding of the biblical writings and who have interest in discovering the manner in which these writings are interpreted in the Christian and Jewish traditions.

In the last quarter century an unprecedented openness and under-standing has emerged among Jews and Christians in the United States. Further, increasingly in recent years, Christians and Jews have moved from *speaking* with each other to *working* together. Although, areas of difference and misunderstanding need continuing attention, inherent in the present speaking-working dialogue is the promise of a shalom relationship between the two communities.

The present volume focuses on the Hebrew Bible/Old Testament, which both Jews and Christians hold to be inspired Scripture; it is a part of this new working relationship between the two communities. Here Christian and Jewish scholars cooperate in the publication of a volume in which they provide commentary on biblical texts out of their own traditions. Similarity and difference are present — no attempt has been made to pro-duce a volume that reflects the lowest common denominator of agreement. Both the unity and diversity, reflected in these text-expositions, witness of the One whom both Jews and Christians praise for divine, life-giving love.

In this ecumenical effort, we are grateful for the encouraging interest and generous support of Dr. and Mrs. Glenn Palmberg, Bellevue, Wash-ington. Also, we thank Ms. Jeanine Brown, Faculty Secretary, North Park Theological Seminary, for her careful and willing work in preparing the manuscript for publication.

FREDRICK C. HOLMGREN AND HERMAN E. SCHAALMAN

Introduction

Every classic text bears an excess and a permanence of meaning that yields new meaning and resists once-and-for-all definitive interpretation. This every scholar of the classics knows. Moreover, every classic text is always highly particular in both origin and expression, yet public — and, in the case of the greatest classics, universal in effect. This particularity every historian and social scientist can show. In sum, the effort to interpret any classic text (as distinct from any period piece) is extremely demanding.

Some great religious traditions (like the classical Confucian and the neo-Confucian) demonstrate this complexity through centuries of rigorous and communal interpretation of their religious classics. Yet, other religious traditions (like Hinduism and some forms of Buddhism) have the even more difficult job of interpreting not merely classics but sacred texts — sacred for and to the religious community. Three traditions — the famous religions of the book, Judaism, Christianity, and Islam — have the yet more difficult task of interpreting texts that are not only religious classics or even sacred texts but, in the strict sense, Scripture.

For two of those communities, Judaism and Christianity, the scriptural texts even receive different names: the 'neutral' scholarly name of the Hebrew Bible, the Tanach of Judaism, and the Old Testament of Christianity.

No texts have received such diverse interpretations from the earliest periods of their formation until today. No texts so well yield the insight into the permanence and excess of meaning of the classic texts and now become the even greater excess of these texts, a testimony to revelation (and at the limit, as in kabbalistic readings, manifestations of God's very reality in the texts). The Jewish and Christian preacher may well feel silenced by the enormous history of interpretations and wholly different methods of interpretations of these scriptural texts that each community names as God's word to us.

Surely preaching attempts the most difficult task of all: allowing that Word of God to come alive anew for a particular congregation at a particular moment in its history. Surely the preacher (I am one) is always searching for good, that is, scholarly and believing, readings of these extraordinary biblical texts. More exactly one searches for words that bespeak a scholarship that employs one of the great secular methods available (historical-critical, social-scientific, literary-critical, etc.), while being informed and indeed (as with several of the amazing scholars in this work) formed and transformed by one of the classic traditional theological approaches: midrashic, rabbinic, kabbalistic, typological, allegorical, "plain sense").

Indeed, I was struck over and over again in reading the clean, clear prose of the scholars of this work of how subtly and seemingly easily they employ both first-rate secular scholarship and exceptional theological and pastoral insight. Each knows that her or his interpretation is not, indeed cannot be, the final word of interpreting some classical biblical text. But each writer calls all of us to sense the sheer disclosive actuality and transformative power of these texts, which we all hope to know better than we do: perhaps as our ancestors knew them; surely as our descendants, we pray, will know them. Thanks to these essays each of us can hear each text with the fresh eyes and the solid scholarship and the pastoral and theological strength of the scholars so carefully chosen by the editors. At times the reader may experience what I did with several of the essays: the sense that I have returned to a text I know I loved and thought I knew only to discover, thanks to the subtle reading before me, that I have returned to a biblical text that was an early love only to see it as if for the first time. The editors and the writers have put us all in their debt for allowing us to hear their learned and pastoral conversations with these classic, sacred, scriptural texts.

DAVID TRACY

The Story of Us All: A Christian Exposition of Genesis 3

ELIZABETH ACHTEMEIER

"Genesis 3 is our story . . . our attempt
to be unqualified secularists."

In order fully to understand Genesis 3 we must understand the context of the chapter. As it now stands, Genesis 3 is part of the Yahwist's primeval history that includes Genesis 2:4*b*–4:26; 6:1-8; 7:1-5; subsequent portions of chapters 7 and 8; 11:1-9, 28-30; and 12:1-3. The Yahwist's work has now been set into the priestly writer's framework that includes Genesis 1:1–2:4*a*, the genealogies of chapters 5, 10, and 11, portions of the flood story, and the Noachic covenant of chapter 9.

The primary purpose of the primeval history is not to explain how the world began, although that is certainly important and basic to the Christian doctrine of creation. Rather, the main purpose of Genesis 1–11 is to tell why it was necessary for God to enter history in about the eighteenth century B.C.E. and to call Abraham out of Mesopotamia (Gen. 12:1-3). Genesis 1–11 represents Israel's reflection on why God created her in the beginning. It reflects her understanding of the meaning and purpose of her life.

Let us look first at the content of the context of Genesis 3. The confession of faith in Genesis 1–2 is that God created the world "very good," giving it order and light and life and goodness. Humans beings are

1

the apex (Gen. 1:26-28) or the center (2:7) of God's creation, with responsibility to their Creator as stewards of the world (1:28), to care for it and prosper it (2:15). In creation, God pours out marvelous gifts on human beings, giving them, in concert with all creatures (Ps. 104:29-30), the breath of life that sustains their bodies (2:7), but, beyond that, also the gifts of beauty in the natural world (2:8-9), their daily preservative and creative work (2:15), their food (2:9), and the joyful union of one flesh in marriage (2:24). Indeed, Genesis 2 understands the body, the desire of the sexes for one another, the mutual helpfulness of husband and wife, and the family resulting from their union all to be gifts of a loving and caring God.

According to Genesis 2:16-17, however, there is a limit placed on human existence, and that limit is symbolized by the "tree of the knowledge of good and evil" that God has created in the garden. The limit has nothing to do with human learning and science. God is not trying to prevent us from exploring in the space age, for example. Moreover, the limit is placed upon human beings out of love, because God does not wish us to die (cf. Ezek. 18:32). But "knowledge" in the Hebrew includes also the ability to do. And the "tree of the knowledge of good and evil" is, therefore, a symbol of omniscience and omnipotence, of the ability to do and to know everything, including right and wrong. In short, the tree symbolizes the ability to be gods. But we are not gods, of course. Human beings are creatures who are totally dependent on our Creator for all good gifts and for life itself.

Genesis 3, therefore, is the story of human attempts to shed the limits of creaturehood, to be divine, to make the Creator God unnecessary, and to be our own gods and goddesses instead, determining for ourselves what is right and wrong, creating our own history and direction and goals, pursuing our own plans according to our own will and purposes. In short, Genesis 3 is the story of our attempt to be unqualified secularists, that is, without God in the world.

Genesis 3 is our story still today, because the writer did not intend for Adam and Eve to be understood as an original, historical couple. 'Adam is the Hebrew word for "man" or "mankind" (or, we would say today, "humankind"). The Yahwist writes the story here of humankind, thus setting the call of Abraham in Genesis 12 against the backdrop of universal history. And the Yahwist intends Genesis 3 to be the story of how we all have walked in relation to God. (Thus, "Adam," in Paul's writings, becomes the symbol of the "old man or woman," in the old age before the redemption in Christ). Genesis 3 is *our* story, the picture of how we act and think. It has no specific historical date; it portrays daily occurrence.

To be sure, Christian theology in the past, for example in the writings of Augustine and Thomas Aquinas, understood Genesis to portray the Fall of our original ancestors, and their concupiscence or original sin was then understood to pass down from generation to generation, corrupting the whole human race. But the real intent of Genesis 3 is to emphasize each individual person's responsibility for the Fall and that person's own rebellion against God's lordship. That rebellion, however, is then understood throughout the Scriptures to affect not only the individual's life but also the life of the world and society and even the cosmos as a whole, as we shall see.

The story begins with a characterization of the serpent as a creature that the Lord God has made. It is, therefore, clear that the serpent, in verse 1, is not intended to be a symbol for Satan or the devil or the "adversary" (cf. 1 Pet. 5:8). The only characteristic that distinguishes the serpent from other creatures is that it is more "subtle" or "wily" than they, and the Yahwist draws upon that characteristic to use the serpent as a protagonist in the story. The serpent is initially a narrative device, nothing more.

The serpent draws the woman into a theological conversation, which, on the face of it, would seem like a desirable act. After all, is it not good to talk about religion and faith and theology? Pastors yearn to engage their parishioners in such discussions. But the conversation turns out to be what Dietrich Bonhoeffer has described as the first conversation *about* God. That is, it is a conversation in which God is an object to be discussed, and that is not at all desirable. God has become here — as in so many theological and religious discussions — an impersonal something, about which the speakers can speculate, over whom they can argue, and toward whom they can be interested or indifferent.

God the object! How strange it is to find that in this story! After all, God is the Creator who has shaped the woman by hand, in the most intimate fashion, as a potter working with a lump of clay (cf. 2:7). God has breathed into her and, indeed, into the serpent the breath of life and sustains them alive every moment with that breath. And God has set them both into a garden that is sufficient for all their needs. But both Eve and the serpent break that intimate, dependent relation with God and turn God into a thing at which to look. Theology that goes that route very quickly gets into trouble.

The trouble immediately follows, and it consists of the serpent setting before the woman three temptations, which parallel the three temptations Jesus faced in his conversation with the devil in the wilderness (Matt.

4:1-11; Luke 4:1-13). The first temptation comes in the form of an innocent question, "Did God say, 'You shall not eat of any tree of the garden'?" (Gen. 3:1). In other words, is God trying to deprive you of something that you need and desire, Eve? Is God, therefore, not good? Will God not let you have those things necessary for your health and well-being and happiness? Think of all the things that could make us so happy — material comfort, success, an easy conscience, good kids, a happy family life, importance in the community, even beauty or a slim figure. And what happens? We keep having bad luck instead, and things don't work out, and God isn't looking out for us, and God's not on our side, and God is not good!

Eve, of course, does not go quite that far. She still has some recognition that God has provided for her. And so she affirms that God has given her food from every tree except from the tree in the midst of the garden. But God has drawn a boundary around her desires, to be sure, and she must not even touch the forbidden tree, she maintains, or she will die (Gen. 3:3).

God, however, has not said that Eve must not touch the tree (cf. 2:17), and so in her reply to the serpent, the woman has exaggerated God's stricture. Indeed, the woman has begun to set up her own little tinny moral code, just as so often we construct such codes in our zeal for our faith: "If you want to be a Christian," we dictate, "you must not do such and such." In short, self-will, apart from the will of God, has entered the picture. The door to rebellion has opened just a crack, and the serpent now sees an opportunity to attack God directly.

Thus the serpent sets before the woman the second temptation, and that is to believe that God is not serious (Gen. 3:4). "You will not die," says the snake. In other words, God does not mean what he says. All of those commandments that God has laid upon us should not be taken too seriously: "Love your enemies"; "Forgive seventy times seven"; "Do not commit adultery"; "Do not covet"; "Unless you turn and become like children, you will never enter the kingdom of heaven"; "Everyone who hears these words of mine and does not do them will be like a foolish man who built his house upon the sand." God cannot mean those things! After all, God loves us, and God will always forgive us, right? God cannot be serious! Surely our faith is not a matter of life or death!

Thus the relation with God becomes a matter of little importance, and when that stage is reached, we take to ourselves the freedom to do whatever we like. And so Eve is now vulnerable to the serpent's third and most serious temptation — to believe that God is not God but little more than a jealous, insecure, arbitrary, and selfish dictator. "God knows that when you eat of it your eyes will be opened, and you will be like God, knowing good and evil" (Gen. 3:5). We can break the bounds of creature-hood and become our own deities! We can be free, self-determining, self-fulfilling agents of our own destiny! The woman has set before her the ultimate temptation of pride.

The subtlety with which the Yahwist pictures our resulting sin in this story is marvelous, for in verse 6, eating the forbidden fruit looks to Eve like the right thing to do at the time. And how characteristic that is of our sin against God! Few of us set out deliberately to do evil. Most of us want to be good, religious people. And the sin that we do looks like the right thing to do at the time; it looks like the loving thing in the situation; it looks like the compassionate thing, the proper thing, or the wisest course of action. The only difficulty is that the act is a violation of God's com-mandment.

But the story pictures our sins of complicity, too. Eve also gave some of the fruit to her husband, and he ate (Gen. 3:6). He just goes along. And so often we just go along. Someone makes a racial slur, and we do not say a word in protest; we just go along. A government structure is totally unjust, and we do not work to remedy it; we just go along. Adam is, indeed, every one of us in this story.

But our rebellion against God's loving guidance always has evil consequences, and in this story those consequences are immediate. The sin of the couple corrupts every good gift that God has given them. First of all, it corrupts their relation with one another (Gen. 3:7). Suddenly they are no longer joined together in a joyful relationship of "one flesh," but now guilt and shame enter their union, and they become self-enclosed egos standing over against one another. "They knew that they were naked," verse 7 puts it — separate, with something to conceal from one another, and something to fear. And so they make coverings to hide behind, flimsy protections against one another. How often we cover ourselves with lies and deceits and rationalizations to protect ourselves in our deepest rela-tionships.

The woman and the man not only have to hide themselves from another, however. Because of their attempt to make God unnecessary, they now have to hide themselves from God (Gen. 3:8) — that God who has created them in the most intimate fashion and loved them and provided all their necessities. Now the relationship with God is broken, and God must go in search of them — a wonderful touch in the story about the ever-searching love of God.

Paul Scherer, the great Lutheran preacher of the past generation, once remarked that we should stop talking about "finding God." "God is not lost!" exclaimed Scherer. "Human beings are lost. The question is not, 'God, where are you?' The question is, 'Adam, where are you?'" And God walking in the garden in the cool of the day — at early morning or at twilight — calls out with that question in the never-ending search for his creatures. "Adam, where are you?" "What is this that you have done?" (Gen. 3:9, 13).

Although we human beings try to shed our relationship with God and to be our own deities, there is no way in which we can rid ourselves of that relationship. We are created in God's image, says Genesis, totally dependent on our Marker, never fully understood except in that dependency, and always unable to escape our tie with our Creator. God will deal with us in love, or God will deal with us in wrath; but one way or another, God will always deal with us, for we are creatures connected with and always responsible to God.

Reinhold Niebuhr used to teach us that "love is the willingness to take responsibility." Love for God is the willingness always to answer to God for what we do; and love for our fellow human beings is the willingness to be responsible for one another. But in this story of us all, we are pictured trying to shed both forms of accountability. When the man and the woman are asked to shoulder the responsibility for their actions, they try to dodge the demand and to pass the buck. How ironic that is! They wanted to run their own lives and to be their own gods and the captains of their own fate, but they will not take upon themselves accountability for their actions. Indeed, they blame everyone but themselves: the woman, God, the serpent (Gen. 3:12-13). "Lord, it's not my fault," they imply.

In his searching book *Whatever Became of Sin?* Karl Menninger wrote that the most important ingredient missing in our society today is the sense of responsibility, and when we read this story in Genesis, we are reminded of all our excuses: "I live in an evil environment"; "My parents didn't raise me right"; "I've got this psychological hangup"; "The alcohol (or drugs) made me do it"; "I was temporarily insane"; "I goofed; we all make mistakes"; "That's just human nature"; "Sorry about that."

But we are responsible to our God, and so the Lord lays judgment upon the woman and the man and the serpent for their rebellion, and that judgment further corrupts the good gifts God has given them.

In verse 14, we find what was originally a little etiological tale about why snakes crawl on their bellies, but in verse 15, the serpent becomes a symbol of something else in this story. It is no longer simply a wily creature among other creatures that the Lord God has made, but the serpent becomes the symbol of that evil that our sin has let loose in the world, a prefigurement of the dark power of what later in the Scriptures is called Satan or the devil, or, by Ephesians 6:12, "the cosmic powers of this present darkness," and "the spiritual forces of evil in the heavenly places."

Moreover, that power of evil, introduced into the world by our attempts to make God unnecessary, takes on a life of its own according to this story (Gen. 3:15), and our existence becomes one of unending struggle with evil, from generation to generation.

The further corruption of the relation between the wife and her husband is detailed in verse 16. The woman has been created to join flesh with her husband in the joyful union of the marital covenant, but now the resulting birth of a child becomes that which gives her pain and threatens her life. And she no longer knows the equality and sharing and mutual helpfulness with her husband that she was given in the beginning (Gen. 2:18; "fit for him" in that verse reads in the Hebrew, "corresponding to him"). Rather, though her desire is still for her husband, he rules over her, and she knows only that humiliating domination against which the women's movement has raised such an agonized cry in our day. The subordination of female to male, this tenth-century story in Genesis states — over against the practice of every other society — is the result of our sinful attempts to shed our creaturehood and to be our own Creators.

God's judgment on the man is equally severe. Creative and preservative work was originally given to the man as a good gift of God (Gen. 2:15), but now the man's labor is turned into drudgery and toil to earn his daily bread (Gen. 3:17-19), and now workers everywhere find themselves leading lives of quiet and futile desperation. The man is never given back for his toil a reward commensurate with it (Gen. 3:18).

Indeed, the sin of humankind corrupts the very earth itself, spoiling God's good gifts of beauty and fertility and replacing them with the thorns and thistles of ugliness and barrenness (Gen. 3:17), a fact we know all too well from the ecological disasters of our time. "Cursed is the ground because of you." Our sin infects the world, so that the apostle Paul could later write that the whole creation groans under the burden of that corruption (Rom. 8:22). Disease, birth defects, genetic maladies, parasites, nature "red of tooth and claw" become the price the creation pays for our sinful rebellion against God.

Worst of all, death is laid upon the face of the earth and becomes the wages of our sin: "You are dust, and to dust you shall return" (Gen. 3:19). The veil of sorrowing and meaninglessness, of void and darkness is spread over all nations and creatures (cf. Isa. 25:7-8). The life abundant that God intended in the beginning is transformed into the *finis* of the grave.

There really is no explanation in this story of *why* we sin against God. The ancient couple, symbolizing us all, have been given every good gift for their life together and singly. They have the freedom to choose, within the wide bounds of their creaturehood. All things are theirs, to enjoy and to preserve. They have almost unlimited possibilities for creativity and work with the world around them. The only thing they have been denied is the possibility of divinity. And the only warning they have been given is not to reach in pride for that status. But reach they do, in violation of their God-given nature, and that brings upon them and all their world corruption and violence and death. The story reads not too differently from our morning headlines.

Why do we try to do without God, who has lavished so much care on us? In Christian terms, why do we turn our backs on the God who loves us and the world enough to send his only Son to die for us in order to give us eternal life? There is no more senseless act than that. Yet, turn we do and walk away from God and journey off into some far country on our own. And we end up, like the prodigal, starved for the bread of life.

No, there is no explanation for sin against God, no reason that can explain it, and this story of us all in Genesis leaves it unexplained — a mystery of our being from the first moment that we draw breath, a temptation ever set before us until the moment that we die. The Bible tells us that the power of that mysterious sin can only be overcome by trust — by trust in the goodness of our Creator God to forgive and to transform and guide our lives; by trust that he means it to go well with us and, therefore, gives us commandments about how to live and the power to obey them. But a child will obey a parent only if the child trusts the parent's love and guidance. At the heart of our faith is the necessity of that trust.

That the love of God is never overcome by our sin and lack of trust is implied by what follows in our story. In sheer mercy, God the Tailor sits down and makes clothes for the wife and her husband in order that their life together may still be possible (Gen. 3:21). Then, too, the man and woman do not immediately die. God's grace overcomes their rebellion and preserves them alive. Indeed, the Lord even helps Eve to escape death when she gives birth to Cain (Gen. 4:1).

But the sentence holds; the judgment is there; the couple is driven out from the garden, away from the tree of life that would enable them to live forever (Gen. 3:22-23). God means what he has said; he is very serious; the garden paradise is lost. And reentry into the garden is blocked by cherubim and a flaming sword (Gen 3:24). Humankind has passed the point of no return; there is a guard at the entrance to the garden; and there is nothing human beings can do to get rid of it. Only God can remove the guard; only God can restore humankind to abundant life.

In the stories that follow in the primeval history, we see the sin we have introduced into the world spread its tentacles out to capture all of creation. In the story of Cain and Abel, in Genesis 4, the sin of the parents infects their offspring and leads to fratricide, so that in punishment Cain is totally alienated from the natural world and becomes a fugitive and a wanderer on the face of the earth.

A little history of the growth of civilization is given in Genesis 4:17-22, but its result is the further disruption of the marital relation by the introduction of bigamy (Gen. 4:19), and the smith's work, according to verse 22, issues in the manufacture of Lamech's terrible sword of vengeance. Lamech becomes the symbol of human hatred for humankind.

In Genesis 6:1-4, the sin has spread to infect even the heavenly beings, so that in the introduction to the flood story, verses 5-8, humankind, that desired to know and to do all things (Gen. 3:5), can now only do evil, and God must make a new beginning with creation through Noah and the rescued species.

After the flood, humankind does not improve, however, for God can still say in Genesis 8:21 that our hearts are evil from our youth. Thus the final picture of our sin is presented in the story of the tower of Babel (Gen. 11:1-9). In that story, our pride has reached its zenith in our desire to create our own fame and security. But that pride leads to the dissolution of community, and we come to the end of the primeval history, in which human sin has taken over the world. That is intended to be the sad story of us all.

Although we have investigated only Genesis 3 in detail, we can point to a pattern that extends throughout these stories in the primeval history. Human sinfulness spreads ever wider in each succeeding story, and God's judgment on that sin is, therefore, ever more severe. But throughout the stories there is always some covering grace — the gift of children to Adam and Eve, the protection of the fugitive Cain, the rescue of Noah and his family and all species of creatures, the promise of Genesis 8:21-22, and finally the renewal of the creation in Genesis 9 and the Noachic covenant. At the end of the story of the tower of Babel, however, any covering grace of God seems absent. Humankind is left under the curse of sin, with all community becoming impossible, the creation and all God's good gifts for life corrupted by our rebellion, and death spread like a mantle over all the face of the earth.

But at Genesis 12 the Lord calls Abraham out of Mesopotamia and gives him a threefold promise: that he will be the father of a great nation, that his descendants will have a land to call their own, and that through those descendants God will bless all the families of the earth. In short, in the historical figure of Abraham, the progenitor of Israel, God begins a sacred history that will reverse the effects of our sin and make abundant life for all once more a possibility.

We have lost our paradise, Genesis says, so God will give Israel a new land, flowing with milk and honey. Human community has become impossible, and so God will make a new community that knows how to live in justice and righteousness under his guiding lordship. We live under God's wrath and curse because of our rebellion against him, and so through Abraham's descendants God will turn it all into blessing.

More than that, according to Genesis 17, God will establish with Israel an everlasting covenant that restores the relationship with our Maker that we abandoned in our pride.

The message, then, of the Scriptures is that God wishes to draw all peoples into that new community of Israel — into the "commonwealth of Israel," as Ephesians 2:12 terms it. Indeed, God wishes to graft even Gentile wild branches into that Israelite root (Rom. 11:17-24). The rest of the Bible tells how God goes about that task, but that is not the subject of this particular essay.

The point is, as we mentioned at the beginning, that Genesis can only properly be understood in the context of the primeval history. And the primeval history can only properly be understood as the preface to the call to Abraham. God calls Abraham out of Mesopotamia in order to restore the fallen creation, whose goodness we have corrupted by our attempts to be our own gods and goddesses. God calls Abraham because we are evil and God is good. God begins sacred history because God loves us all.

Cain and Abel: Bible, Tradition, and Contemporary Reflection

GUNTHER PLAUT

What role does God play in the
occurrence of violence and injustice?

I consider the biblical story of Cain and Abel to be one of the most compelling found in the entire Torah. The story works on many levels, and once you explore it fully it will stay with you as a warning and a question.

The story first. We meet two brothers who, according to the biblical text, are the first offspring of humanity's original forebears, Adam and Eve. I do not take this story literally in the sense that we all are descended from one single pair of human beings, whose name the Bible has preserved and with whose children we are dealing in detail. To me, as to most modern readers, the opening chapters of Genesis and especially this story deal not with historical figures but with mythic people: they are people who — because they are portrayed as among the first to walk on earth — incorporate in their lives some of the traits we find in ourselves. Telling their tale also answers some questions about our own existence, which is the subject of my abiding interest in biblical tales in general and this one in particular.

Cain and Abel then are representatives of a human family, any human family. They are siblings who are most likely near to one another in age and who are competing with each other. In the setting of the tale, both are pictured as trying to win God's favor; they bring a sacrifice, but for reasons that the story decides to hide, God favors Abel over Cain. Here is the text:

> Now the man [Adam] had intercourse with his wife Eve and she conceived and bore Cain. . . . she then bore his brother Abel. Abel became a keeper of sheep and Cain became a tiller of the soil.
>
> In the course of time Cain brought an offering to the Lord from the fruit of the soil and Abel for his part brought the best of the firstlings of his flock. The Lord paid attention to Abel and his offering, but to Cain and his offering he paid no attention. Cain was greatly distressed, and his anger mounted. Thereupon the Lord said to Cain: "Why are you distressed, and why is your anger mounting? Do the right thing and everything will turn out alright. But if you do not do the right thing sin is lying in wait at the door and its urge is fastened upon you. There is still time to master it."
>
> Cain argued with his brother Abel, and when they were in the field Cain set upon him and killed him.
>
> The Lord said to Cain: "Where is your brother Abel?" and he responded: "I do not know. Am I my brother's keeper?"

The story then goes on to tell us that God condemned Cain and made it impossible for him to till his soil; the very earth was cursed under his feet. So Cain became a wanderer across the face of the globe. Later we read that Cain founded a city somewhere in the land of Nod, east of Eden.

The story has many layers, and each one speaks to us in a different voice. In order to approach it properly we have to do what we ought to do with every biblical story (in fact, with every old text): we must read it on three levels.

The first level is what we call the historical or antiquarian where we ask the question: How was this text first heard? How was it experienced? How was it understood? To answer that question we have to know something about the setting and the time in which the story was composed and what its references might have been. Sometimes we find that the words themselves had one meaning in ancient days and a different meaning later. (Examples from any language can illustrate this point. In Shakespeare's time the word *knave* simply meant a youthful attendant to a knight; today it conveys a sense of moral deficiency. A generation ago, the word *gay* conveyed an attitude of joy; today it primarily denotes a male homosexual.)

The second level is the level of tradition. There we ask: What have the centuries made of it since the first hearing of the story? What traditions have developed around it, what meanings have been added to or extracted from it? That tradition reaches from the ancient days to yesterday, and its contributors are not only the ancient rabbis but also the interpreters of other religious traditions like Christianity and Islam. In addition, there are philosophers and poets, believers and unbelievers, and all of them have in their way contributed to enriching the text. The ancients might not recognize their interpretation, but that does not matter.

And third, there is your understanding and mine or anyone's who reads the text. We may understand it the way the ancients did, or tradition may speak to us on one level or another, and then again it may speak to us in a totally new voice. That is the great attraction of the Bible. As we read it and reread it, it shines to us like a prism that we turn as the light refracts through it, ever new colors playing upon our retina.

So I suggest that we read this story now on the three levels and see what it tells us.

Level one. How did the ancients when they first heard the text (for they did not read it, most of them being unable to read) understand the story?

They understood it to be, in part, a reflection of family life, a sibling rivalry with disastrous consequences. No doubt many a family could then (as now) identify with such a scenario: one child being preferred over the other by a parent who does not explain such preference.

But they also heard something else in the tale, and I think it is this understanding that gave it its original impetus. Note that Abel became a keeper of sheep, a herdsman, a nomad or semi-nomad, and Cain became a tiller of the soil, a farmer. Read the story on this level and see it as a conflict between two of humanity's basic civilizations, the nomad and the farmer. These two basic occupations of antiquity coexisted for a very long time until somewhere around the thirteenth or twelfth century B.C.E. an industrial revolution took place. The Late Bronze Age gave way to the Iron Age. The reason: people learned how to manipulate iron, cast it, mold it, and shape it. The most immediate and revolutionary consequence of this invention was the creation of the plow. With that invention much of humanity transformed radically. Now farming became ever more widespread, people laid claim to the soil, and where the herdsmen had been able to roam freely, they now came up against land claims and fences, with signs posted metaphorically or otherwise: So far and no further! Private property. One hundred years later people would ask: What ever happened to the shepherds that roamed our country? The answer would be, to use a modern idiom, "The farmers killed them."

This was most likely a major theme that was readily understood. Once upon a time, so stories and legends went, nomads had roamed the earth with their flocks; now they have all but disappeared, and the farmers have their claims staked out and are in sole possession of the land. The Cain and Abel story gave this development a literary framework. Every once in a while people still surface in biblical tales as people coming from the outside, people with tradition of the desert and the herdsman. Moses is one of those examples; he comes to attack an established civilization as one who has learned his world view in the loneliness of a shepherd's life.

But he is an exception; the community was not composed primarily of farmers and city dwellers who made up the polity. Abel is dead, and, as the biblical tale goes on, we learn that — speaking in metaphor — he is being replaced by Seth, the new man. Cain may have been punished by having to leave that which he loved most, his own possession, his soil — but he turned his talents to another pursuit: he founded a city. That, too, reveals an ancient judgment that persists into our own time. That brief statement (Gen. 4:17) tells us what many ancients thought about the city: it was the seat of evil, of corruption, prostitution, greed, and all the other negative aspects of the age. To some degree that tradition still remains alive in many lands. The countryside is where the good people live. They have decent morals, a healthy outlook on life, and the farmers' families are close to one another and help each other. But the city, that is where corruption begets a thousand vipers, and that is where much of what is bad in our society is seen to originate. And if you ask, why would this be so? you should not wonder: the person that invented the city is none other than the murderer Cain. What murderers have wrought cannot be good. So much for level one. This, I think, is what the ancients heard first and foremost, along with the theme of sibling rivalry, which is ageless.

Level two. In later centuries, the struggle between nomadic and agricultural civilizations was all but forgotten, and now that tale was heard and read in a different way. Now the emphasis was on the dialogue between God and Cain: What have you done and where is your brother Abel? Whereupon Cain professes his ignorance and responds contemptuously (one can almost see him shrugging his shoulders): "How would I know, am I my brother's keeper?"

This answer became the theme that tradition took up and with which no doubt most readers of this story were raised. Although God does not answer the rhetorical question of Cain, the punishment is swift and sure, and thereby God gives answer: You are your brother's keeper, every person is responsible for everyone else. Society is one single unit, and no one stands apart. Tradition read the story as one of social responsibility. Jewish tradition, with a special emphasis on the Jewish community, phrased it memorably: "All Jews are responsible for one another."

Level three. How do you read the tale? Does level one appeal to you or level two? Or is there something else? Is there perchance another dimension?

There is, and it is found in the Midrash, which ascribed a particular interpretation to a sage who lived in the second century. It did not become a popular interpretation, for reasons that will become apparent at once. For many a year I had known it, but it did not speak to me with any insistence. Then, one day, it did, and thereafter it became my preferred reading of the text. It did not speak to me of sibling rivalry, nor of the farmer versus the shepherd, nor of social responsibility. All these were present, but there was a meaning that for me was more important than all the others.

Here is how Rabbi Shimon bar Yochai understood the text. God asks Cain about his brother Abel, and Cain asserts his ignorance. More than that, he argues with God, and by turning the tables he says to God: You ask me where my brother Abel is, and I ask you, don't you know? Am I alone my brother's keeper — aren't you as well or perhaps more so than I? You are God, and I am only human.

Rabbi Shimon then goes on to this frightening analogy. He compares God to the emperor who watches gladiators fighting in the Colosseum. Aren't you, God, like the emperor watching the two men fight, and when one is about to be overcome he has one last chance to appeal to the mercy of the emperor who watches the game from his royal box and who, by raising his thumb can give him life or, by pointing it downward, decrees his death? Says Cain to God: You turned thumbs down on Abel when he cried to you in his agony and now you blame me and you ask *me,* "Where is your brother?"

Note that God really doesn't answer the question. It is as if Cain had silenced the divine voice, and in fact God preserves Cain's life and merely makes him homeless. Somehow it appears that the theme of God's co-responsibility runs through the tale. For our generation this has a macabre attraction, for, to put it in modern words, Cain asks the Auschwitz question. Where was God when the condemned cried for life and were not heard?

Did God turn thumbs down on them as, in Rabbi Shimon's Midrash, God turned down thumbs on Abel?

The implications are clear. The question was asked then and it is asked today and the final answer has still not been given. Religious people still struggle for an explanation of God's silence. So did Rabbi Shimon, and he ends his reading of the text by saying: It is better to put one's hand on his mouth and be silent too. Better we should not pursue this theme.

Rabbi Shimon's reading of the text does not leave me alone. On the third level the text speaks to me of human beings searching for God among the apparent injustices of life. Where does God's power end, where does it begin? The question remains open.

This is how I now approach the fourth chapter of Genesis. All three levels have something to contribute to my understanding. I listen to it with the ancient ear, I listen to it with the ear of tradition, I listen to the voice of Rabbi Shimon. Severally and together these voices convey the rich fabric of this text. This text demonstrates the multilayered meanings of the Bible, and as we look at them level by level, they make it abundantly clear why this is indeed the Book of Books.

What Is "This" They Begin to Do?

KATHLEEN A. FARMER

*"Is 'this' an attempt to be like God
or to avoid being like God?"*

The narrative popularly called the "Tower of Babel" story is short and sweet (only nine brief verses in modern versions and 121 words in the Hebrew text), but it is far from being simple. In fact, the text of Genesis 11:1-9 is a carefully crafted and highly polished narrative artifact. Close analysis of the rhetorical, stylistic, and structural elements of the text provides ample evidence that the story is a tightly woven work of art.[1] The action in the story is neatly balanced: the first four verses refer to human action, the last four to divine reaction. In the first half of the story, humans plan their actions with the phrases "Come! Let us" (do this) and "Come! Let us" (do that), and in the second half of the story God plans the divine reaction with the very same opening phrase (Gen. 11:7). The center verse in the story acts as a point of intersection between the two realms of action, when Divinity "comes down to see" what on earth humankind is doing (Gen. 11:5).

---

1. The summary that follows depends primarily on Isaac M. Kikawada, "The Shape of Genesis 11:1-9" in *Rhetorical Criticism: Essays in Honor of James Muilenburg* (Pittsburgh: Pickwick, 1974): 18-32, and J. P. Fokkelman, *Narrative Art in Genesis: Specimens of Stylistic and Structural Analysis* (Assen/Amsterdam: Van Gorcum, 1975): 11-45. But see also Umberto Cassuto, *A Commentary on the Book of Genesis, Part Two: From Noah to Abraham,* trans. Israel Abrahams (Jerusalem: Magnes, 1964): 225-49.

The narrator plays with the sounds of the original language: the words translated "there" (used once in vv. 2, 7, 8, twice in v. 9), "name" (vv. 4, 9) and "heavens" (v. 4) have very similar sounds in Hebrew (*sham, shem, shamayim*). The consonant sounds *B* and *L* (the key sounds in the words for "babble" and "Babel") occur repeatedly in various combinations throughout the story, referring to both human construction (*nilbenah,* "let us make") and divine obstruction (*nabelah,* "let us make meaningless"). Alliteration and assonance of sound combine with symmetry of construction in communicating the meaning of the whole.

It seems reasonable to conclude, on the basis of such evidence, that the words and phrases of the text have been fitted into the narrative picture like tiles in a mosaic floor. Thus it comes as a bit of a shock when we find that, in the midst of this carefully controlled communication, the *cause* of God's displeasure is left undefined.

Look again at verses 5 and 6. The text actually says that when the Lord came down to see the city and the tower that the children of humankind had built, the Lord said, "Look! One people and one language for them all, and this they begin to do. And nothing keeps them from doing all they plan to do."

"This they begin to do," and the Lord sees "this" as an ominous sign for the future, but what does "this" mean specifically? To what does "this" refer? Anyone wishing to preach or to teach from Genesis 11:1-9 must surely supply a logical antecedent for "this." But even those who have meticulously analyzed the language, the syntax, the rhetoric, and the structure of the text can come to essentially opposite and incompatible interpretations of the story. Thus, for instance, Kikawada concludes that the scattering of the people is an act of grace or a means of blessing on the Lord's part,[2] while Fokkelman argues that it is an act of retaliation or a means of punishment.[3] Since the antecedent of "this" is not specified, the story as it stands in the canon is inherently multivalent: it is open to more than one appropriate reading. Readers are virtually forced to go beyond the boundaries of the pericope in order to find clues with which to make sense of the Lord's displeasure. However, the immediate literary context of the story (the primeval history in Genesis 1–11) provides interpreters with at least two very plausible but contrary potential solutions to the problem.

2. Kikawada, 32.
3. Fokkelman.

Is "This" an Attempt to Be Like God?

According to the majority of modern interpreters, God's displeasure is caused by human *hubris;* human pride, presumption, arrogance, and self-exaltation are often named as the "sin" to which "this" refers. And "scattering" is seen, in the eyes of the majority, as God's punishment for such rebellion.[4]

Some readers think the people's plan to build "a tower with its top in the heavens" is tantamount to rebellion.[5] The apparent meaning of the name *Babel* ("gate of God") in the Babylonian tradition inclines many to see the building of the tower as a struggle for power. It is said that the people want to set themselves up as rivals to God or that they want to gain access to God on their own terms rather than on God's terms. Various interpreters see "this" as an attempt to storm the gates of heaven, to flout the authority of God, or to disrupt the God-given order.

Other commentators call the people's desire "to make a name for themselves" sinful: it is a mark of their overweening pride, indicative of their search for security apart from God. The condemnation of "this" in the story should remind us that only God can give human beings a name that really matters (cf. Isa. 56:5). Those who argue in this direction can

4. Gunther W. Plaut, *Genesis: Commentary* (New York: Union of American Hebrew Congregations, 1974): 106. This is not merely a modern opinion: early Haggadic interpretations depict humankind rising in actual revolt against the Lord. However, an extensive (though not exhaustive survey) of major commentaries on Genesis published in English since 1960 indicates that at least the following can be named as proponents of this interpretive option: Umberto Cassuto, *A Commentary on the Book of Genesis, Part Two: From Noah to Abraham,* trans. Israel Abrahams (Jerusalem: Magnes, 1964); Robert Davidson, *Genesis 1–11.* Cambridge Bible Commentary: New English Bible (Cambridge: University Press, 1973); Everett Fox, *In the Beginning: A New English Rendition of the Book of Genesis* (New York: Schocken, 1983); John Gibson, *Genesis,* Daily Study Bible Series (Edinburgh: Saint Andrew Press, 1981); Michael Maher, *Genesis,* Old Testament Message, vol. 2 (Wilmington, Del.: Michael Glazier, 1982); Gerhard von Rad, *Genesis,* Old Testament Library (Philadelphia: Westminster, 1972); Ephraim Speiser, *Genesis,* Anchor Bible, vol. 1 (Garden City: Doubleday, 1964); Bruce Vawter, *On Genesis: A New Reading* (Garden City: Doubleday, 1977); Gordon J. Wenham, *Genesis 1–15,* Word Biblical Commentary, vol. 1 (Waco, Tex.: Word, 1987); Claus Westermann, *Genesis 1–11: A Commentary,* trans. John J. Scullion (Minneapolis: Augsburg, 1984).

5. The popular name for the story in Christian circles indicates the centrality of the "tower" motif in traditional interpretation. In contrast, the early rabbis referred to it as the story of "The Generation of Separation" (Genesis Rabbah 38:1-10).

point to the next story in Genesis for support. After humankind has been thoroughly scattered over the face of the earth for having tried to make a name *for themselves,* God calls Abraham and tells him, *"I* will make of you a great nation, and *I* will bless you and make your name great . . ." (Gen. 12:2; emphasis added).

Fokkelman concludes on the basis of his detailed analysis that "Yahweh finds himself confronted with unexpected concentration of power, with a revolution which threatens to subvert the cosmic order created by him."[6]

Readers who understand the ambiguous phrase in verse 6 to mean human *hubris* (whether they see it manifested in the building project or in the search for "a name") may defend this interpretive resolution by appealing to the third chapter of Genesis. The "temptation" to which humankind succumbs in Genesis 3 is traditionally interpreted as the "sin" of trying to be "like God" (Gen. 3:4). The Lord is traditionally thought to have been distressed by human attempts to be like God, the Lord seems to have seen some ominous potential in the "godlikeness" of humankind (Gen. 3:22), and the Lord seems to have responded to this potential threat by sending humanity forth from the garden of Eden (Gen. 3:23).

Fokkelman also appeals to the flood story and its prelude as a precedent for this reading of the Lord's character: "When in Gen. 6 the human race degenerated and was going to be a threat to God, by relationship by marriage with 'sons of God' among other factors, he struck back, wiping out everything. . . ."[7] The remarkable symmetry of syntax and vocabulary in the Babel story reminds Fokkelman of the symmetry of *ius talionis* (the principle of equivalent restitution or equivalent retaliation) as illustrated by Genesis 9:6, which he translates, "whoever sheds the blood of man, *for* that man shall his blood be shed."[8] Thus Fokkelman sees the scattering of humankind by means of the confusion of tongues as a form of divine retaliation, illustrating the principle that the punishment should fit the crime.

6. Fokkelman, 27.
7. Fokkelman, 31.
8. Fokkelman, 35.

Or Is "This" an Attempt to *Avoid* Being Like God?

A small but persuasive interpretive minority[9] argue that the people in the Babel story have not set themselves up as rivals to God at all. Quite the contrary, in fact. If "this" refers to an act of rebellion, it is a form of rebellion that grows out of insecurity and fear rather than out of pride or ambition. Advocates of this interpretive option appeal to the first rather than to the third chapter of Genesis. Thus, for example, Kikawada points out that the phrase translated "upon the face of all the earth" clearly ties Genesis 1:29 to the Babel story.

> Our understanding of the meaning of the story is supported further when we view it in its larger context. Within the primeval history of Genesis 1–11, our story unit as described above may be argued to form the conclusion, constituting an inclusio with the beginning, Genesis 1.[10]

The creation story that stands in our completed canon as an introduction to everything else tells us that God created humankind in God's own image on the sixth day, just before God took a well-deserved day of rest. The narrator emphasizes that this act of creation had a specific purpose or function: "God blessed them, and God said to them, 'Be fruitful and multiply, and fill the earth and subdue it; and have dominion over the fish of the sea and over the birds of the air and over every living thing that moves upon the earth'" (Gen. 1:28).

The command to fill the earth is closely tied to the concepts of image and dominion. To have dominion means to take responsibility for. It does not mean to exploit for one's own benefit. In Israel, as well as in other parts of the Ancient Near East, the ideal ruler was understood to be a caretaker, responsible for the well-being of all the subjects under his or her dominion. Furthermore, it was the custom in most of the Ancient Near East

9. Walter Brueggemann, *Genesis,* Interpretation: A Bible Commentary for Teaching and Preaching (Atlanta: John Knox, 1982), presents the most complete and detailed recent exposition of this interpretive option. See also Donald E. Gowan, *Genesis 1–11,* International Theological Commentary (Grand Rapids: Eerdmans, 1988); W. Gunther Plaut, *The Torah: A Modern Commentary* (New York: Union of American Hebrew Congregations, 1974); Eugene Roop, *Genesis,* Believers Church Bible Commentary (Scottdale, Penn.: Herald Press, 1987); Nahum Sarna, *Understanding Genesis* (New York: Schocken Books, 1970).

10. Kikawada, 31.

for rulers to have images or likenesses made of themselves. Images were sent to the far-flung corners of the realm to represent the rulers and their interests in absentia. The images played a significant part in the ruler's dominion.

Thus the initial chapter in the primeval history implies that God created and sent humankind forth to multiply and fill the earth in order that they might act as the images of God, representing God's presence and upholding God's interests in the far-flung corners of the world. We may conclude from Genesis 1 that God wanted humankind to fill the earth with God's own image in order that God might better exercise dominion over all creation.

Subsequent chapters in Genesis tell us how God eventually found it necessary to purge and cleanse the world of evil. But after the Flood, God blessed Noah and his children once again and said to them, "Be fruitful and multiply and fill the earth" (Gen. 9:1). In Genesis 9:6, the survivors of the Flood are reminded once more that God made humankind in God's own image before they are commanded yet again to "be fruitful and multiply, abound on the earth and multiply in it" (Gen. 9:7). Immediately after the end of the Noachic story comes a genealogy followed by the final story in the primeval history, which tells us that the children of Noah got sidetracked in their travels and decided they would rather settle down comfortably together than be scattered over the face of all the earth.

Thus it may be argued that the key to understanding the ambiguous "this" lies not in the people's actions but in their explicitly expressed motives. A close look at verse 4 indicates that everything the people planned to do (both their building projects and making a name for themselves) was directed toward one end: to *avoid* being scattered over the face of all the earth. When the Lord came down to inspect the city and the tower that the children of humankind had built, the Lord said "Hmm . . . here we have one people and one language for them all, and *this* is what it leads to. As things stand right now, nothing keeps them from doing what they *plan* to do . . ." (emphases and translation mine). What did they plan to do? They planned to avoid being "scattered abroad over the face of the whole earth" (Gen. 11:4). As Brueggemann points out, the verb *scatter* is the common element between the human proposal (Gen. 11:4), the divine action (Gen. 11:8), and the conclusion of the story (Gen. 11:9).[11]

If the command to scatter in Gen. 9:1-7 is tied to the purpose of

11. Brueggemann, 98.

creation "in the image of God," then it is clear that the people were under-motivated rather than overly ambitious. The problem, according to this minority viewpoint, is not that the people have arrogantly tried to be like God but that they have tried to *avoid* being godlike. God has had to take corrective action because humankind has tried to avoid carrying out the very mission for which they were created in the first place.

Further support for this latter reading can be drawn from the interplay of words within the construction of the story itself. If we assume that Genesis 11:1-9 is a tightly woven piece of narrative cloth, then we must consider the possibility that the repetition or even the placement of words and phrases within the story constitute part of the message the final editor intended for the audience to receive. In fact, the story begins and ends with the exact same phrase: "all the earth" (*kol ha'arets*). In nine short verses (only 121 words in the Hebrew text), "all the earth" occurs five different times (once in vv. 1, 4, 8, twice in v. 9). The Hebrew word for *one* is used four times, the word for *all* is used seven times. Thus it may be argued that the story moves from the homogeneity of *one* to the diversity of all, from a people clustered together in *one* place to people scattered over the face of all the earth. The narrator's chosen vocabulary contributes to the interpretive conclusion that it is the self-serving unity of the people, "a unity grounded in fear and characterized by coercion,"[12] which motivates the Lord's response.

However, the idea that the people's naive ambition to build a tower "with its top in the heavens" is an attempt to storm the gates of God's realm is not supported by the actual language used in the text. The tower is mentioned only twice, both times in connection with the city, and it is not mentioned at all in the conclusion of the story. The text only says that when the Lord scattered the people abroad, "they left off building the city." The building of the tower per se thus seems to have had little to do with the main point of the story.

From Exegesis to Sermon

I have argued above that the ambiguity of "this" in verse 6 forces us to look outside the text of the story itself for clues to guide our evaluation of the people's action and the Lord's response. And I have demonstrated that

12. Brueggemann, 100.

the immediate literary context of the Babel story provides us with at least two quite plausible (though contrary) possible ways of reading "this they begin to do."

It might be argued that both interpretive options could be subsumed beneath the larger heading of "rebellion against the created order" or "rebellion against God's will for creation." But if a sermon is to speak meaningfully to a modern audience about modern mores, some conclusion must be reached concerning the nature of this rebellion. The preacher must decide (at least provisionally) what this rebellion against the created order might look like in contemporary terms.

Fokkelman concludes that the narrator "teaches his listeners and readers a lesson: these people are bad examples: let them be a warning to you, do not be over-bold if you want to be spared God's punishment, know your place and do not be so self-sufficient. . . ."[13] In other words, it sounds like a sermon based on the *hubris* resolution of "this" might appropriately be titled, "Don't Get Uppity with God!" But Brueggemann concludes that "the scattering God wills is that life should be peopled everywhere by his regents, who are attentive to all parts of creation, working in his image to enhance the whole creation. . . ."[14] A sermon based on this interpretation might appropriately be titled, "Be All That You Are Made to Be!" Is there any way to determine which is the better choice?

The Implicit Assumptions of the Options

It seems to me that an interpreter's inclination to favor one option over another grows out of the prefabricated (a priori) assumptions each of us brings with us to our readings of any text. Every reader inevitably brings theological and cultural presuppositions to the reading of a text. The interpretive option that explains "this" as "incipient Titanism" (humans setting themselves up as rivals to God) assumes either that God is jealous of the divine prerogatives or that God's security is threatened in some way by human endeavors. It is possible, of course, that at some level in the development of the canonical text the narrators did read God's character in this way. It is, after all, possible to distinguish various layers of intentionality in the history of this text. At some stage in its history, the story was

13. Fokkelman, 42.
14. Brueggemann, 99.

apparently an etiology: an attempt to explain how there came to be so many different languages on earth. At some stage in its development this story may have been a polemic against the arrogance of city-state empires. In some stage of its growth it may have served as an ethnic joke, satirizing the Babylonians who gave the Israelites so much grief by capitalizing on the similarity of sounds in Hebrew for the word meaning babble and the name Babel. If the motif of human hubris plays a part in the story at all, that part belongs to an early stage in the redaction of the text.

In the formation of the biblical canon, each of these recognizable levels of intention has been caught up in the larger, more complex intentions of the Scripture as a whole. I have to admit at this point that one of the assumptions that I bring to the interpretive task is the assumption that the inspiration of Scripture is located in the final, canonical level of the tradition.[15] I assume intentionality at every level of the development of the canon. (In other words, I assume that the earliest speakers of the earliest forms of the Babel story intended for their listeners to understand something specific from their utterances. I assume that those who collected these utterances and handed them down or wrote them down or included them in their larger literary contexts did so with a purpose in mind.) But I expect to find God revealing God's self to people of faith today only in interaction with the final form and content of the whole biblical tradition.

I find it hard to believe that the God we worship and in whom we place our trust is displeased when humans try to take the initiative in divine-human relationships or that God punishes us whenever we try to be like God in some way. Thus I come to the reading of the text predisposed to question whether the final level of the redaction of the Babel story actually upholds this reading of the character of God (as one who feels threatened and retaliates in response to a human assault on the divine prerogatives). Is it merely wishful thinking on my part to assume that the actions of God in the Babel story are open to another legitimate reading? Is it "eisegesis" if we read Genesis 11:1-9 with the assumption that God is secure in the superiority of God's own power and that God's merciful, creative, and redemptive purposes (those qualities of God revealed to us in a particularly vivid way in the person and work of Jesus Christ) have always played a part in God's dealings with humankind? Or does the text as it now stands, in its final level of redaction, actually allow us to see

15. See Paul Achtemeier, *The Inspiration of Scripture: Problems and Proposals* (Philadelphia: Westminster, 1980): 134-36.

God's displeasure with human actions here as a part of God's creative and redemptive nature? Is it possible to see the scattering of humankind in this story as a redemptive rather than a punitive measure?

The story tells us only that the actions of the remarkably unified descendants of Noah somehow displeased the Lord. When the Lord came down to see the city and the tower that they had built, the Lord acknowledged that there was great power inherent in human unity: "They are one people and they have all one language; . . . nothing they propose to do will now be impossible for them" (Gen. 11:6). Thus it is quite possible to say, on the basis of the text itself, that it is not merely their potential power as a unified group but the fact that they are using this power to circumvent God's plans that displeases the Deity. There is logical, internal, and contextual consistency to support the argument that God feels the need to put a stop to "this" not because God's superiority is threatened but because God knows that if all the humans who reflect God's image cluster together in one place, if they do their best to avoid being scattered over the face of all the earth, then God will be under-represented in the far-flung corners of the universe.

When understood in this way, God's scattering action does not appear to be retaliation or punishment for human sin. It is, rather, God's way of encouraging humankind to carry out God's intentions. There is nothing in the story itself or in its immediate context that mitigates against reading God's purposes in this story as merciful, creative, and redemptive. Why, then, have so many interpreters opted for the "Don't Get Uppity with God" point of view? I suggest that many interpreters in the modern world come to their reading of the biblical texts assuming that the hierarchically structured societies in which they live and work are earthly reflections of a metaphysical reality. When the jealous guarding of privileges and prerogatives by those in positions of power and authority is the norm in human society, it is relatively easy to invest God's actions with analogous motives. Or, on a more personal level, it is relatively easy for those of us who are the parents of teenagers to imagine a divine parent feeling threatened by rebellious children. Most of us also find it difficult to conceive of scattering as a positive rather than a negative action on God's part. We think of togetherness and unity and cooperation as virtues in human communities. We work long hours to build close-knit groups in our churches. In fact, we have to think hard to come up with conditions under which the breaking up of community and the scattering of people to the far corners of the earth could be considered gracious or redemptive actions.

But if we take seriously the full context in which the Babel story is now found, then we will be forced to remember that the story of the working out of God's purposes in the world neither begins nor ends with the confusion of languages. Christian interpretation usually links the Babel story with the story of Pentecost, reminding us that in the story of the whole, the confusion of languages is merely one episode along the way that leads eventually to a day when people speaking different languages hear the good news of God's redemptive purposes proclaimed in each of their native tongues (Acts 2:5-11). The story of the whole reminds us that the good news began to be spread across the face of the earth by those who were "scattered because of the persecution that took place over Stephen" (Acts 11:19) and that these early preachers were not particularly anxious to be scattered either. They were inclined to want to talk only to people who held certain ideas in common with themselves (Acts 11:19). It seems to have come as something of a surprise to them to find that speaking to people of different languages and cultures had such positive results, "so that a great number became believers and turned to the Lord" (Acts 11:21).

How a preacher chooses to preach from Genesis 11:1-9 will depend a great deal upon the assumptions he or she ordinarily makes concerning the nature and purposes of God. But the choice of an appropriate sermon topic also depends upon the preacher's reading of the nature of the congregation to which she or he speaks. Since the ambiguity of the language in Genesis 11:6 makes it possible to preach either repressive or liberative messages through the medium of a single story, the burden of choice rests heavily upon those who preach. What is it that your listeners need to hear in order to restore them to a proper relationship with God?

My own reading of the climate in the average American church today leads me to believe that in terms of what God created us all to be there are far more underachievers than overachievers in our pews. There are far fewer images of God in the world, taking seriously their God-appointed responsibilities for the well-being of creation, than there ought to be. When I look around in my own life in the world today, when I examine my own inclinations and listen to others around me expressing theirs, I conclude that human nature has not changed very much between the time of the Babel story and our own time. We human beings still tend to prefer the familiar comforts of being around people who are like us — people who "speak our language" (however *language* may be defined). We still prefer to group ourselves into cozy, homogeneous communities where we can build various kinds of walls around ourselves in order to avoid being scattered abroad into unknown, unfamiliar, and, therefore, uncomfortable places.

But when I read the Babel story in its larger context, assuming that God's redemptive intentions are the same today as they were then, I am forced to conclude that God does not intend for us to gather ourselves into safe, harmonious enclaves where everyone speaks the same theological or spiritual or political language. God does not want us to cluster tightly together in comfortable groups where everyone thinks alike and talks alike, where all our collective energies are devoted to the avoidance of disturbing or scattering influences. When we do so, we are going against God's plans for us.

Genesis 11:1-9, taken in the context of the whole Scripture, clearly recognizes the power inherent in human unity and the potential for disaster inherent in the misuse of such unity in attempting to subvert the purposes of God. But the eleventh chapters of Genesis and of the book of Acts proclaim the same God, whose plans for humankind have not changed. This God does not intend for us to cluster together in homogeneous groups, nor does this God intend for us to proclaim the good news only among those who speak our own language. Rather, the God we worship and whose good news we proclaim wants us to "fill the earth" with the images of God in order to represent God's interests in every far-flung corner of the universe. But unlike those early settlers in the fertile plains of Shinar, we need not be afraid to scatter, for the Scriptures as a whole inform us that scattering at the Lord's behest is a calling, not a curse.

Boldness in the Service of Justice

LOU H. SILBERMAN

"Abraham cannot save the cities . . . but,
like Job, he has saved God."

The story of Abram/Abraham that begins in the twelfth chapter of Genesis with what could not have been other than a shattering command: "Go forth from your native land and from your father's house to the land that I will show you," and through a variety of changes and adventures comes at last to a quiet end in Genesis 25: "And Abraham breathed his last, dying at a ripe old age, old and contented; and he was gathered to his kin," that story has, as a whole, long captured my imagination. Year after year, as the lessons containing it are read, I am ever finding something new and unexpected to join what the past years have already disclosed. I have traveled with him and his caravan as they have trekked the wasteland; gone down with him into Egypt where he all but lost his beloved Sarah; fought the battle of the kings and encountered that strange priest-king Melchizedek. I have watched the awesome making of the covenant; beheld the three strangers appearing over the horizon; listened to Sarah's embarrassed tittering behind the curtain; and shuddered to the very center of my being at the altar on Mount Moriah. I have seen him mourn the passing of Sarah and have traveled with his servant to distant Aram in search of a wife for Isaac his heir. I stood by the cave of Machpelah as his sons, Isaac and Ishmael, together for a moment, laid him to rest.

Which among these many tales has called for my attention above all others? What impresses it ever more deeply into my thoughts? Why is this story of Abraham's reckless confrontation of the Divine so challenging? I turn to it once again, seeking the answer to my own question.

We are at the entrance of Abraham's tent by the terebinths of Mamre as he rests in the heat of the day. Suddenly he sees three men standing nearby, and running to greet them he bows down. Here the Midrash, the interpretations of the early generations of the rabbis, intervenes. [Midrash will intervene often in this essay, for studying it has been my preoccupation for more than a quarter century.] The previous chapter had ended with the account of the circumcision of Ishmael and had noted that Abraham was ninety-nine years old when he was circumcised. Is there not, perhaps, a connection between the chapters? a rabbi asked. Abraham was convalescing from the operation when the strangers appeared, yet the duty of hospitality was such that, discomfort aside, he hastened to attend to his guests.

Hospitality was a sovereign demand in Abraham's world, but there was one occasion when he failed to live up to his duty. There is an Islamic story from Persia that tells of that event (Benjamin Franklin knew it and published it as the fifty-first chapter of Genesis): Abraham was sitting before the entrance to his tent when an old man wandered by. Without a moment to spare, Abraham rushed out to him. "Ancient one, turn aside into my tent; bathe your tired feet; rest a while and join us at our meal." And so it was. When they had sat down, without a word the man reached out, grabbed some food, and began to eat. "Father," said Abraham, "I should think that a man as advanced in years as you and undoubtedly filled with respect for the divine giver of our food would say a word of thanks, not to me but to its gracious giver." "Not so," replied the man, "I know nothing of such behavior. We fire-worshipers have no such practice." "Fire-worshiper," cried Abraham, "leave at once! You will not eat under my roof!" And he drove the old man out into the night. Later, as he slept, the Lord came to him in a dream. "Abraham, for over eighty years I have borne with that man. Could you not have done so for one night?" Perhaps it was in remembrance of that failure that ninety-nine year old Abraham rushed to his task.

This is only the beginning of what is for me the compelling center of the narrative. There is, to be sure, the promise of a son to be the bearer of the blessing. I have often wondered about Sarah's thoughts at the time. Was she wrong in laughing to herself? Perhaps she nodded her head knowingly and mused, "Men . . . men." Was not her laughter a premonition of the fulfillment of the promise, their son, Isaac (i.e., laughter) for "God has brought me laughter." After this the men set out on their journey toward Sodom with Abraham seeing them off. Suddenly the narrative comes to a halt; we are taken into the divine confidence: "Shall I hide from Abraham what I am about to do?" Yet, before we have been made privy to what it is, the Lord muses on his relation to Abraham and what he wants of him and his descendant: "to keep the way of the Lord by doing what is just and right" (v. 19). We ought to mark these words for they are crucial to the tale. Only now do we learn what is on the Lord's mind. It is "the outcry that has reached" him from the cities of the plain.

Once again the Midrash instructs me how to read the text. The Hebrew word translated as "the outcry" is a noun with a feminine possessive pronoun attached so that it can, grammatically, be translated "her outcry." It is just this that Rabbi Levi does. In typical midrashic fashion that can see in such a small grammatical feature a wealth of meaning, he has the Lord reflect: "Even if I wished to hold my peace in the case of the young girl, I would not allow myself to do so." What was the case? Rabbi Levi elaborates. It was the case of two young girls who went down to the spring to fetch water. Said one to her friend, "Why do you look so ill?" The other replied, "We are without food. We are near to dying." What did her companion do? She filled her own jar with grain and exchanged it for her friend's. When this became known, they took her and burnt her. Said the Holy One blessed be He: "I will never allow myself to ignore the case of the young girl." This is why it is written: "her outcry," not "their outcry." Thus I begin to understand what the words "just and right" intend. I am not called to respond to some vague generalization concerning human suffering; I am called to attend to the outcry of the young girl; the outcry of that single person in distress.

How necessary this is in the world in which we live. It is not "they" who are starving in Ethiopia; it is that child with a bloated belly who stares out at us from the television screen. It is not "the homeless" who wander our streets; it is that man who has lost his job, his home, his family, his hope. Now I am close to the heart of the tale. The narrative resumes. The men descend toward Sodom while Abraham remains there looking down at the cities of the plain. He knows what they are. He knows the corrupt lives their inhabitants lead. He knows without being told what is in store for them, what the Lord has planned. But he does not stand there with bowed head, acquiescent to the divine will as he perceives it. No! But now must I search for the right word to set forth Abraham's stance. The word I prefer is the Hebrew *chutzpa,* but what English word will say it? *Temerity?*

Audacity? Insolence? Impudence? Impertinence? They all say too much.
Would *cheeky* do? Hardly. Perhaps *boldly* is the most appropriate term.
Indeed, there is a story reported in the Palestinian Talmud that demonstrates
how boldness in approaching the Divine can, on occasion, be a virtue.

What a scene! Abraham standing there looking out at the cities, aware
of what is in store for them, knows what the Lord wants of him: "to keep
the way of the Lord by doing what is just and right." He knows, too, what
he wants of the Lord. "And Abraham went forward." Some rabbis discussed this phrase. One said that the term "go forward" means going to
war. Another said that it refers to conciliation. A majority thought that it
meant going forth to pray. We may ask, did he not go forward to ask from
the Lord that which the Lord required of him, "doing what is just and
right?" The confrontation begins at once, for there are no words of greeting,
only the incredulous question, "Will you sweep away the innocent along
with the guilty?" This is the way we read it, and properly so. Nonetheless,
the Midrash offers us another insight. The question is posed in another
way. By means of it Abraham tells the Lord what is involved in his
contemplated act. "Will you allow your anger to sweep away the innocent
along with the guilty? You are in control of your anger; your anger is not
to control you." How is it possible so to understand the text? By reading,
as one rabbi did, the Hebrew word *haaf,* which we understand as an
interrogative, as a substantive, *haaf,* meaning anger, for the two words are
homonyms and in the consonantal Hebrew text may be read in these two
ways. Another rabbi, reading the word in the same way, has Abraham
saying to the Lord, "If you bring anger into the world you will destroy the
righteous together with the wicked. Is it not enough for me that you refrain
punishing the wicked for the sake of the righteous rather than destroy the
righteous together with the wicked?"

Abraham pushes further. Spare the city for the sake of only fifty
innocent. "Far be it from you to do such a thing, to bring death upon the
innocent as well as the guilty, so that the innocent and the guilty fare alike."
Then again the impassioned cry. "Far be it from you!" Twice we hear,
"Far be it from you!" What is Abraham demanding? Our translation
undercuts the agony of the phrase, for the Hebrew has within it the meaning
"to defile," "to profane." As an ancient teacher said: Abraham declares
that such an act would be a double profanation of the divine name. The
Lord by such an act will sully his own name and reputation in the world.
In our tradition there is no sin greater than the profanation of God's name,
and that profanation occurs not through words but through deeds. It is

human action, acts of a person toward another, that defiles the name. Abraham will not allow the Lord in anger, righteous though it be, to act in such a fashion as to bring contempt upon the divine name. God would be seen as the deity who slaughtered the innocent together with the guilty!

Then the question of questions: "Shall not the Judge of all the earth deal justly?" Is this really a question? Is it not a demand echoing as it does the divine demand upon Abraham's posterity, "to keep the way of the Lord by doing what is just and right"? These are shuddering words, this human demand upon the divine. It is the same demand that Job, in his suffering, made: Where is God's justice to be found? In the human world, were a judge to err there is always the possibility of appeal. To whom, to what can we appeal against the divine decree? Only to the quality of justice itself. Find fifty, Abraham urges. But how in such a city are fifty to be found? The solution: there must be, says a rabbi, at least enough good deeds among them that, added all together, are the equivalent of fifty. If not, he has Abraham plead, "You who are the righteousness of the world, add your righteousness to their paltry good deeds to make the fifty."

Remarkably, this rabbi seems to turn the words inside out. The Judge of all the earth cannot do justice. If, he has Abraham say, you desire the world to endure, there cannot be strict justice; if there is strict justice, the world cannot endure. You have seized hold of both ends of the rope. You want the world to exist and you want justice. Without your giving up a little, the world cannot survive. To this the Lord replies by quoting Psalm 45:8, "You love justice and hate wickedness," and then interpreting it, "You seek to justify my creatures; you hate to condemn them, therefore has God, your God, chosen to anoint you with oil of gladness over all your peers. There are ten generations from Noah until you, yet you alone did I call into remembrance." It seems that Abraham's demand has been granted. The presence of the innocent will save the wicked. Yet, there is more to it. Time and time again Abraham, fearfully — "I who am but dust and ashes"; "Let not my Lord be angry if I go on" — but boldly nonetheless — "I venture again to speak" — furthers his demand. Fifty? Fifty lacking five? What of forty? Thirty? Twenty? Even ten? Each time there is the divine acquiescence, "I will not destroy."

At the end, Abraham cannot save the cities, not even if the ten are found in them, but, like Job, he has saved God, for he has reminded God of God's own decision at the very instant of creation. A Midrash notes that the first verse of Genesis states, "When God [Elohim] began to create," while verse 4 of chapter 2 reads, "When the Lord God [YHWH Elohim] made heaven and earth." Why the difference? The answer lies in the distinction between the two names of the Deity. Elohim is, in the traditional interpretation, the name of divine justice; the tetragrammaton, YHWH, is the name of divine mercy. Before the words of creation were spoken Elohim intended to bring the world into being under the attribute of justice but recognized that it could not endure, so Elohim set the name of mercy, YHWH, before the name of justice, Elohim, and created the world as Lord God (YHWH Elohim). This insight is set within a parable: "This is similar to the case of a king who possessed fragile cups. He pondered, if I pour hot liquid they will shatter; if I pour in cold, they will crack. What did he do? He mixed the hot and the cold together and they remained intact. So, too, the Holy One blessed be He said, 'If I create the world under the attribute of mercy its sins will be many; if under justice, how can it exist? I can create it with both and may it endure.' "

My teacher Julian Morgenstern raised this issue in another context that supports the midrashist's reading of the text. He put the matter in terms of the covenantal relationship between the Lord and Israel. They were bound together by mutual promises. Obligations, the commandments, had been offered to Israel by God, and Israel had accepted them. That acceptance had brought forth the responsive obligation of God to Israel. They had become God's people who were to fulfill the obligations they had accepted. The Lord was their God, their sovereign, who would lead, guide, and protect them so long as they remained obedient. But as the prophets proclaimed over and over again, Israel had been faithless, had broken the covenant. God was thus freed of the obligation. How and why could and should they remain God's people? Repudiate them! Let disaster come! It is deserved. True, disaster came, but not repudiation. Why? That was the question the prophets pondered. Justice, strict justice, required that the faithless not only be punished but be cast aside. Yet, it did not happen. Why? For Isaiah it was God's *hesed* that intervened. What a wondrous word this is: mutual obligation, friendship, solidarity, loyalty, fidelity, generosity, graciousness. One cannot, dare not choose among them in this setting. It is all of these and more. This is why, Isaiah recognized, the rejection he proclaimed on God's behalf cannot, will not happen. *Hesed* overrides strict justice. For Jeremiah it is much the same, "That is why my heart yearns for him; I will receive him back in love" (31:20). Ezekiel sees the divine name as the motive at work. For the sake of all that the Lord intends for creation, all must see and recognize that the people of God is not a failure to be rejected but a promise yet to be fulfilled.

What does this chapter do? It opens up in a wonderful way the relationship between human and Deity. The Divine trusts a human. "Shall I hide from Abraham what I am about to do?" This is no arbitrary Deity acting without concern for humans. This is, in Abraham Joshua Heschel's phrase, "God in search of man." And the human trusts the Divine and thus dares to face God boldly. "Here I venture to speak to my Lord, I who am but dust and ashes." Together the Lord God and humans struggle with a world in which justice and mercy are intermingled, striving for a world in which, at last, mercy, YHWH, alone shall be the Divine name. As Zechariah proclaimed: "On that day the LORD (YHWH) shall be one and his name one" (14:9).

The Binding of Isaac

HERMAN E. SCHAALMAN

*"Not only did God test Abraham, but . . .
Abraham also tested God."*

Few passages in the Torah can match the intensity of the drama and meaning and none exceeds the account in Genesis 22 of the binding of Isaac, *akedat yitzchak*. Let us note at the very beginning that tradition does not speak of the sacrifice of Isaac but of his being bound. And while it might be said that tradition reduces the otherwise unbearable tension of the commanded offering up of Abraham and Sarah's only son, it is truer to the eventual outcome of the story.

One might claim that that outcome was already foreshadowed in the opening words: ". . . God tested Abraham." And one interpretation of this phrase would imply that God hoped Abraham would pass that test successfully whatever was the point of that test. Abraham's readiness to obey God even when commanded to offer up his son Isaac might have been anticipated in his willingness, demonstrated much earlier, to surrender to God's call to leave behind everything he knew and cherished and to entrust himself without reserve to the voice that had enticed him: "Go, go from your land, from your birthplace, from your father's house to a land which I will show you."

Little doubt here that Abraham was prepared to follow this newly revealing God unquestioningly, though even then the keen ear of traditional interpreters could hear an otherwise unreported reluctance: "from your land, your birthplace, your father's house." They detected in this progression "land," "birthplace," "father's house" the divine overpowering of an Abraham who step by step wanted to make sure that he had heard correctly and that God was, indeed, inviting him to forsake his entire background to embark on a radically new and different experience: "A land which I shall show you. . . ." It could not have been more vague and indistinct but also more enticing.

Abraham had been willing to follow that divine voice, apparently the first ever to do so, for we might well assume that God had called many others before Abraham who had refused to hear and listen. If, then, God had tested Abraham in Ur of the Chaldees and found him responsive, it might be assumed that the same God calling again and commanding another impossible act from his new covenantal partner should find him similarly willing.

Yet, there remains a nagging question concerning this testing by the God of Abraham. Does the Torah want to suggest that God was unsure of Abraham's reaction? Did God really not know how Abraham would respond? Is God not supposed to be omniscient, that is, truly all-knowing, hence also able to foreknow Abraham's reply, and thus omnipotent in being able to force Abraham's hand?

There is a radical difference between omniscience and omnipotence. God may know all but may not be able to compel compliance. Or, to put it differently, from God's angle of view awareness may be total for all we know, but from a human point of view such awareness not only is never attainable, is not part of human experience, but is virtually beyond our imagination. We might be able to state that God knows all, but we can really in no way plumb the true depth of that statement. Surely Abraham did not know whether God had foreknowledge of his response to the divine command. And foreknowledge was really not the issue.

What God wanted was an act, the offering up of Isaac. Abraham, awakened from a deep sleep to be told to bring Isaac as an offering, also did not know, at least for a moment, how he would respond.

He had answered *hineni*, here I am, surely bewildered, partly disoriented, trying to figure out what he was being told to do, trying to make sure that it was God who had called. There are possibilities, after all, as suggested by some commentators, that it might have been Satan who was playing tricks on him. Some commentators say that during his three day journey Satan whispered to Abraham not to listen, not to obey, to declare himself unwilling to accept the monstrous demand of offering up his son

Isaac. Yet, having said *hineni*, here I am, he had really committed himself, had placed himself at God's disposition of him no matter how startled and initially tentative his awakening response may have been.

He had said *hineni*, here I am, a second time when his son, breaking what had been an unbearably silent journey, addressed him: "Father!" Only this *hineni* was measurably different from the first. Here his son broke into that heavy silence, the inescapable reflection of Abraham's profound unease, his continuous inner struggle as to whether he was doing the right thing, whether he should really go ahead with God's command or turn around and refuse to comply. This *hineni* was meant to reassure his son, to show Abraham's readiness to acknowledge Isaac's presence, to give him to understand that he sensed his son's perturbed state of soul. The silence, after all, must have hung heavily between them, probably unusual and ominous. Abraham may even have been relieved that Isaac had addressed him, though his brief reply did little to reassure Isaac and, on the contrary, may have reinforced his sense of foreboding. But, again, he was not evading, not hiding; he was there, *hineni*, here I am.

There had been a third *hineni*. When God's angel cried out to Abraham to stay his hand and spare his son he had also answered *hineni*, here I am, only this *hineni* was one of profound relief, of the almost unbelievable reprieve. Three times the text reports that he had said *hineni*. Each had been under such significantly different circumstances that, though he used the same word, each reflected an entirely different mood and set of soul.

This account's assertion, ". . . and God tested Abraham," is certainly true for Abraham; but in a very significant way it was also true for God. We may state categorically that God knows all — but with one exception, the acts of human beings. We experience ourselves as endowed with freedom of will. We know ourselves capable of following God's command and expectations or disobeying and thus disappointing them. We know ourselves to be in a measure free even from God, precisely from God. Why else would there be commandments to do and not to do if we were not free and God wanted us free? God made us free and wants us to be free. That profound, basic fact was established at the very beginning, with Adam, who promptly used this innate, distinctive, and unique capacity of freedom, so totally different from the condition of all other created items and beings, to disobey God.

Or, to put it differently, God took the radical risk in creating Adam that there would now be a creature who willfully, freely, would either be with God or against God or indifferent to God. The test of Abraham, then, is real, is not a pretense or cruel game played by God. God really cannot know what Abraham will do. God can foresee all the many options resulting from the commandment to offer up Isaac, but God cannot know which of these Abraham would choose. It is a real test.

We might still ask, however, why this test was necessary? What did God need to know about Abraham that made it necessary to test him so painfully? Had Abraham not proven to be a worthy, reliable covenant partner of God? Could God not trust him to have those qualities that would make him the root of that people who later became the people of the covenant? Well, perhaps not. God might have detected a defect, a flaw in Abraham that drove God to subject him to the ultimate test, the offering up of his son Isaac. How so?

"And it happened after these matters . . ." so our chapter begins. Tradition came to the conclusion that these prefatory words portended weighty, often painful events to come, that in referring to something in the past they intended to prepare us for dire consequences.

What were "these matters" preceding Abraham's being tested? It was the episode of the expulsion of Hagar and her son Ishmael by Abraham who did so at Sarah's bidding because she wanted this concubine and her son removed from her sight as told in chapter 21. Sarah might have had sufficient provocation to demand what could have been a near fatal removal of these two members of the household, had they not been saved by a miracle. Abraham and she had been unable to produce children. She had finally offered him her handmaid who promptly proved his virility, thus reassuring him, in the birth of his firstborn Ishmael, named significantly "God hears."

Abraham's self-esteem was thus secure; Sarah's was not. On the contrary, Hagar's continuous presence made her an evermore unbearable reminder of her own lack of ability to conceive. And when, finally, the miracle occurred that she conceived and bore a son, an event so implausible that it took an act of divine annunciation to vindicate it, Hagar and Ishmael's presence was a festering thorn in Sarah's side. When, therefore, she had a reason to demand their removal she did.

Abraham was so deeply wounded and upset by this request of Sarah and so unwilling to comply that he consulted God as to what he should do. He heard God say to him: "Do as Sarah requests" and yielding to this divine endorsement of Sarah's demand drove out Hagar and Ishmael into the desert. He did so despite the fact that Ishmael was his firstborn and

Hagar the woman who had authenticated his manhood. We may assume that Abraham did so most unwillingly and in great pain. So, why did he do it? Why did he not assert himself? Why did he not challenge not only Sarah's right to request this removal but also God's advice to listen to Sarah's unreasonable wish? After all, once before he had questioned God's intentions. He had challenged God's plan for the destruction of Sodom and Gomorrah: "What if there should be fifty innocent within the city; will you sweep away the innocent with the guilty?"

It was a bold, unprecedented act. No one before had felt emboldened to question directly the intentions of God. No one had the *chutzpah,* the audacity and courage to confront God from a human point of judgment and imply that God ought not to proceed with the announced plan to destroy these wicked cities. He had, almost foolhardily, sought to bargain with God over the fate of two cities whose evil had, in God's judgment, rightly doomed them to destruction. And while he had become aware of how daring his behavior had been — ". . . I venture again to speak to my Lord . . ." — he had, nonetheless, persisted in his bold advocacy of these unworthy cities. He had given up only when at the number of ten possible innocent to be found there, God broke off this astounding encounter by leaving.

Well, if Abraham had been moved to confront God over Sodom and Gomorrah and, in a manner, to challenge God's wisdom and right to execute their destruction, is it not reasonable to assume that he would make a similar response when confronted with his wife's demand to get rid of a handmaid, his concubine, and his older son? Why, when God advised him to listen to Sarah, did he not rear up and say no? Why did he not question God's justice in this case as he had so boldly earlier: ". . . shall not the Judge of all the earth deal justly?"

As we read the text we can only conclude that he simply gave in. He stood up neither to Sarah nor to God. One might have expected differently. It was not altogether in character for the champion of Sodom and Gomorrah so apparently meekly to yield in the case of his firstborn and his mother. It was "after these matters" that God tested Abraham. He had acted in a manner that might have raised a doubt also in God's mind as to his true nature. If Abraham was to become the ancestor of a people who, because of its covenant with God, would be tested over and over again in excruciating ways, then God needed to be sure that Abraham was in fact capable of passing ultimate questions of faithfulness and obedience.

Accepting for the moment God's necessity of testing Abraham, we cannot avoid the possibility that this test was really reciprocal, that it was two-sided, that not only did God test Abraham, but that Abraham also tested God.

First, the finely tuned ear of the traditional interpreters caught the curious sequence, "Take your son, the one you love, Isaac . . ." and read into it the astonished, wounded retreat by Abraham who did not want it to be true that God was ordering him to offer up the only son of his and Sarah. "Take your son . . ." "I have two sons," commentators report him as objecting. "Your only one . . ." "He is the only son of his mother!" "The one you love . . ." "I love them both!" "Isaac." Now he was caught. There could be no escape or avoidance any longer. It was as he had feared all along. Isaac was God's intended victim.

Was this God's revenge for his having expelled Ishmael without resisting God's words? Was God now taking the remaining son from him in punishment for not having vigorously protected his firstborn? How could God demand this of him who had barely emerged from the grief over the loss of his other son? How could he understand and trust this God who seemed to have encouraged him to give in to Sarah's caprice and now was inflicting a final wound on him? What had God meant when earlier the promise had been given that Isaac was to become his heir, the future of his and Sarah's life, their continuity? He had entrusted himself and his destiny to that God in Ur. He had believed God about the covenant, about the possession of this new land, about becoming a mighty nation. But all of this depended on Isaac living beyond Sarah and him. And now that very same God who had made all these earlier solemn promises was asking for the sacrificial death of Isaac! He really could not comprehend all of this. He was overwhelmed by the ultimacy of that catastrophe that loomed before him. What did God have in mind? How could he, possibly, understand God's workings? He was thoroughly confused. He needed to probe God's will and intent. He, Abraham, had to test God, as it were.

The opening words of our text cut both ways. True, God needed to test Abraham to make sure that he was fit for his ultimate destiny; but Abraham, likewise, needed to ascertain what God really wanted from him and for him. And just as God could not know how Abraham would respond and could not but be reassured by Abraham's ultimate resolve to go through with this horrendous demand, so Abraham, driving the issue to its final climax of being willing to slay Isaac, tested God and found that the earlier assurances were, indeed, valid and permanent. "He stretched out his hand, took the knife to slay his son, and the angel of God called out to him: Do not stretch out your hand against the lad and do him no harm."

If we had any real question or doubt that the Torah implied that God really needed to test Abraham because he could not foretell his compliance, the text settles the matter: "Now I know that you would not withhold your son, your only one from me." Now God knew, not before. Now God could be sure, but not before the test. God, as it were, had learned something.

Likewise, Abraham. He now knew that the earlier promise concerning Isaac was true, reliable, firm. There was to be continuity and future.

Set on bringing an offering to God, Abraham found a goat conveniently caught nearby in a thicket to serve as a substitute for his son. In three days of virtually silent travel through the desert he had brought himself to the point of being willing to sacrifice his son, if needed, to go through with such an offering. Now, God provided and accepted a goat instead. It is the conclusion, the completion of a sequence that until the last moments seemed headed toward radical catastrophe. It closes this incredible, pain-laden episode.

Or perhaps it did not. The conclusion of our Torah passage states: "And Abraham returned with his two servants to Bersheva. And Abraham dwelled in Bersheva." There are, at least, two remarkable omissions in this wording. The returning party comprised three people. Abraham and the two servants. Conspicuous by his absence is Isaac, leading one daring medieval commentator to suggest that God's angel came too late, that Abraham had gone through with the sacrifice, and that Isaac had, in fact, been slain by his father, thus requiring a later miracle of resurrection in order to lead smoothly into the following chapters that pertained to Isaac's life and fortunes.

Aside from this elaborate, astounding flight of fancy one could, of course, come to the simpler conclusion that Isaac after his father's near murder of him no longer wanted any contact with him. Isaac's absence from the text is implicit evidence of a break between son and father that never healed. Isaac never sees his father again. There is no mention of Abraham, for instance, when Isaac marries Rebekah, whom, significantly, he takes to his mother's tent. His father is here nowhere in evidence though he had sent his trusted steward Eliezer to find the wife for his son and thus, indirectly, had been the cause for Isaac's receiving Rebekah as his spouse.

One of the traditional interpreters suggests that Isaac's absence from the text can be explained by his attendance at the *yeshiva,* the academy of his ancestor Er. After all, where would a nice Jewish boy go when he is absent from his father's house?

That Isaac bore the stigma of his father's near sacrifice throughout his entire life is attested by his generally passive demeanor. He is the one patriarch who is more victim than actor, more recipient of his fate than active producer or participant in it. In a way, then, he never recovered from having been bound. All of this is truly remarkable when we consider that according to tradition he was not a small boy, as a quick reading of the text might suggest. He was a man in his thirties when the fateful journey to Mt. Moriah occurred. Or, to put it differently, the aged Abraham, himself well past a hundred years old, could hardly have overpowered an unwilling, resisting Isaac, bound him, and heaved him on top of the altar to slay him. Isaac must have allowed it, must have collaborated in his own sacrifice. He must have finally understood the real purpose of the journey of which his father would not speak either while riding or at the nightly campfires, and only gave the tersest reply, "God will furnish the lamb for the sacrifice," when Isaac, sensing the incongruity of the absence of the offering, had asked, "Where is the lamb for the sacrifice?"

Isaac had really been Abraham's "son," had let his father live up to and act out his understanding of the obligation imposed on him by his having entered the covenant with God. Isaac had been willing to confirm and establish Abraham in his unprecedented role and identity. Without Isaac's tacit complicity Abraham could never have been in a position to fulfill God's command to offer up Isaac. So great was Isaac's love for his father and so great his grasp of the strange bond between God and Abraham.

All the more tragic, then, the evidence of his passivity, his status as a victim as it emerges from the text describing his later life. The experience of being bound apparently broke his spirit. It left an indelible, irreparable mark.

The other equally conspicuously absent person is, of course, Sarah herself. Not only is there not a word of her being notified, let alone consulted, when Abraham took her son away, but there is no word about her when Abraham returns to Bersheva. The next time Sarah's name appears in the text is after her death. "It was told to Abraham that Sarah had died." And where? In Hebron! Are we not entitled to assume that Sarah had left Bersheva before Abraham's return? Apparently she had moved away and gone by herself, though surely not without suitable companions, to Hebron, which was a considerable distance from Bersheva. To put it in contemporary terms, Sarah separated herself from her husband who had become repulsive to her because, as she pieced it together, he had been willing to take away her only son for God knows what dark purposes.

They probably had never really been a happy, congenially married couple. Sarah surely never forgot and probably never forgave her husband for requesting her to declare herself his sister instead of his wife because of his fear that the Egyptian officials, wishing her for their Pharaoh because of her beauty, would kill Abraham if they knew he was her husband. She had been compelled to become part of Pharaoh's harem mostly because her husband refused to acknowledge her as his wife, which might have saved her from such a fate. It was a deeply humiliating experience for her to be treated as a sex object, traded away by her husband fearful for his life. And while she understood and apparently agreed to the need for this deception, she could not help but be profoundly wounded by it. Perhaps her inability to conceive was her unconscious response to what she had to understand as a shameful betrayal. Her departure for Hebron, her virtual divorce from Abraham, and her later lonely death were evidence of the devastating failure of her marriage and loss of her son. There is no word of her ever seeing Isaac again.

The binding of Isaac had left Abraham with neither sons nor wife. No matter that he had passed God's test; his family was in shambles, his life in tatters.

Is this the reward for submitting oneself to God's testing and passing it successfully? Did the father of the covenantal people, himself a covenant partner of the covenantal Lord, deserve such a fate? Painful questions these, leading to the query whether the covenant is a prize or a burden, a blessing or a destiny to be born stoically. Probably both are true, and at the same time. Covenant is a gift but also an obligation, it is an act of grace by a loving God but also a task difficult if not impossible to carry out adequately. It is a boon but also a fateful burden. Abraham began to understand all this though often his biological and spiritual descendants throughout history often forgot this lesson. To be God's people is at least as much the impossible task as it is the blessed evidence of God's grace and love.

Abraham was the first in that tradition, in that understanding of this inevitable ambivalence of knowing God and becoming God's covenantal partner. His acceptance of God's promise is ours, but so is his pain and woundedness. Abraham experienced and came to understand that God is not an easy partner and that it is not easy to enter into partnership with God. But Abraham learned and teaches that the only worthwhile life is achieved through such bonding with God. Isaac lived and handed on the painfully gained, ever enlarging insight into that bond out of which flowed and continues to flow impulses of justice and love, of visions of healing and peace that are the heart of so much human striving and hope.

After Sarah's death Abraham married again. Some traditional commentators claimed that he found and took back Hagar and produced other sons. It was as though he restored her and himself to their erstwhile relation. He died "fulfilled," his turbulent life stilled. He was buried in the same cave that he had bought to bury Sarah with whom he was thus reunited in death. He was buried by his two sons, Ishmael and Isaac, who apparently were reconciled over their father's grave. Thus the Abrahamic cycle ends with every breach headed and every wound closed.

Divine Wonders Never Cease: The Birth of Moses in God's Plan of Exodus

LAWRENCE BOADT

"By becoming a microcosm of the people of Israel itself, Moses is now readied for the task God will give him."

Story and Message in Exodus 1–2

There is never a lack of drama in biblical narratives, but it is rarely fully appreciated. This is especially true for rabbis, pastors, and teachers who must interpret biblical stories in sermons, spiritual conferences, or the classroom. Too often we treat the Scriptures as sourcebooks for beliefs or ethical reflections.[1] We pore over, examine, even analyze texts carefully for their message content, and often spend considerable time seeking out contemporary applications of the message we have found. Both Jewish and Christian students of the Bible are far more likely to treat it as a textbook than an exciting adventure story or source of entertainment. Yet, one could argue that we would get far more message from biblical nar-

---

1. For a scholarly discussion of the relationships between exegesis and doctrines in the interpretation of Scripture, see Raymond E. Brown, *Biblical Exegesis and Church Doctrine* (New York/Mahwah: Paulist Press, 1985), esp. pp. 8-53.

ratives if we did treat them primarily as literary masterpieces rather than as catechisms.

The opening of the book of Exodus is a case in point. The first two chapters are usually treated from perspectives other than the one adopted in the story line itself. Thus early Jewish tradition, represented by Philo, Josephus, and the Midrash Exodus Rabbah, heighten divine intervention and the moral nobility of Moses, the great lawgiver of Israel.[2] In turn, New Testament references emphasize similarities between the role of Moses and the role of Jesus as deliverer and savior[3] and particularly imply that Moses, like Jesus, was rejected by his people but empowered by God to save them nevertheless (Acts 7:23-29; Heb. 11:24-28).[4] Furthermore, the New Testament sources for these stories were closer to the versions of Philo and the Midrash than to the text of Exodus itself. Finally, modern Christian commentaries have focused primarily on the historical reliability of the traditions behind the text of Exodus 1–2, their prior sources and theological development.[5] Often these chapters were treated as a mixture of vague historical recollections, folktale motifs, and editorial reflections. Little was said about the intense wonder and foreboding sense of dramatic change in fortune that these few passages create by their sequencing and development, as well as by the images and themes they employ. Yet, this kind of literary approach to the text may prove the most helpful to a modern audience in recovering the faith dimension that the text conveyed for the ancient authors and their audience.

A fresh look at the narrative as story may unlock a more effective way to read Exodus 1–2 for modern audiences who are sensitive to the interplay of people and events that involves the ambiguity and subtlety that

2. See Philo, *The Life of Moses,* I.1-14; Josephus, *Antiquities of the Jews,* II.9-11; *The Midrash,* ed. Maurice Simon and H. Freedman, vol. III, "Exodus" (London: Soncino Press, 1939): 1-43. Much of this material can also be found in Louis Ginzberg, *The Legends of the Jews,* vol. II (Philadelphia: Jewish Publication Society of America, 1910; reprint 1964): 245-302.

3. See Matthew 2 and the discussion in Brevard Childs, *The Book of Exodus,* Old Testament Library (Philadelphia: Westminster Press, 1974): 20-22, and in Raymond E. Brown, *The Birth of the Messiah* (Garden City: Doubleday, 1977): 228-30.

4. Childs, *The Book of Exodus,* 33-40; also A. T. Hanson, *Jesus Christ in the Old Testament* (London: SPCK, 1965): 82-85.

5. Examples include Martin Noth, *Exodus: A Commentary,* Old Testament Library (Philadelphia: Westminster Press, 1962): 19-28, Ronald E. Clements, *Exodus,* Cambridge Bible Commentary (Cambridge: Cambridge University Press, 1972): 6-17; J. Philip Hyatt, *Exodus,* New Century Bible (London: Oliphants, 1971): 18-49.

often coexist with decisive action in life. Several commentaries in recent years have followed such an approach, stressing the narrative power of the text plot and seeing it in the context of the larger biblical setting (primarily the book of Genesis) and making wide use of comparative literature of Egypt and Mesopotamia. This trend is found among Jewish and Christian scholars alike: Umberto Cassuto, Nahum Sarna, Brevard Childs, Terrence Fretheim, and others.[6] It proves a fruitful collaboration between the two sister faiths that descended from the Hebrew Scriptures.

The Structure of Exodus 1 and 2

Chapters 1–2 of Exodus stand apart somewhat from the central action of liberation that follows in chapters 3–19, a unit that is initiated by the summons of Moses at the burning bush and completed by the arrival of the Israelites at that very same site in chapter 19. Instead, the two opening chapters form a prologue that sets the scene for Moses' call in the wilderness of Midian and establishes the reasons for his mission. This does not suggest that they are extra chapters or unnecessary — without the staging of Exodus 1–2, the succeeding drama of liberation would make no sense. These preparatory scenes need to be taken very seriously as carefully constructed and thematically important elements in the overall narrative of Exodus 1–19. There are seven scenes in chapters 1–2, and they can be divided as follows:

A. 1:1-7   A summary of how the Israelites prospered and multiplied in Egypt over a long period of time.
B. 1:8-14   A sudden change brought a new Pharaoh and oppression by forced labor. Still they multiplied.
C. 1:15-22   Pharaoh plots to kill off all the boy babies and stop their multiplying, but midwives foil him.
D. 2:1-10   The baby boy Moses is born, hidden, and discovered by Pharaoh's daughter — and lives in Pharaoh's house!

6. Umberto Cassuto, *Commentary on the Book of Exodus* (Jerusalem: Magnes Press, 1967); Nahum Sarna, *Exodus,* JPS Torah Commentary (Philadelphia: Jewish Publication Society, 1991); Terence Fretheim, *Exodus,* Interpretation: A Bible Commentary for Teaching and Preaching (Louisville: John Knox, 1991); Brevard Childs, *The Book of Exodus* (Philadelphia: Westminster, 1974).

E. 2:11-15   Moses is outraged by his people's slavery and kills an Egyptian. But now his own people don't trust him.

F. 2:16-22   Moses flees and becomes an exile in Midian, is welcomed as an Egyptian, and settles down as a shepherd.

G. 2:23-25   A summary of the suffering of the Israelites and the long passage of time while God prepares to act.

A. 1:1-7: God's Blessing in Egypt

Section A links us back firmly to the major themes of Genesis. It is unified by its double reference to the "children" of Israel, first in verse 1 where it signifies the literal twelve sons of Jacob, and then again in verse 7 where these have become a nation that is Israel. Between the two reference points the text notes that the growing family of Jacob numbered 70 people, the same symbolic number used of the entire world's population of seventy nations in Genesis 10. Thus we move swiftly from one immigrant family to the readiness of a whole people to take its place among the nations of the world. The wording of promise from Genesis is also used effectively here. The initial account of Jacob's household reflects the promise to Jacob in Genesis 35:11-12, 23-26 in which both the command to be fruitful and multiply and the promise that they would be a great nation are combined with the same enumerated order of the sons. The final verse echoes in very close citation the blessing to be fruitful and multiply given to all creation in Genesis 1:28 and 9:1. So on this level, too, the scene moves from the particular household of Jacob to the world stage.

B. 1:8-14: The Initial Stage of Oppression

Section B of the narrative picks up the theme of section A that the people of Israel grew many and strong (Exod. 1:7 and 2:9). Indeed, the theme of multiplying despite the efforts of Pharaoh to outwit them seems to emphasize the permanence of God's words to the ancestors in Genesis and to set the following events in a context of who is wiser: Pharaoh or those who follow the divine promise. This is confirmed by the repeated suggestions that this people will fight and then go up from the land. Scholars have argued over what this last phrase might mean, but it is best taken as a hint of what is to come. Another hint is the fivefold reference to Israel's hard "service" (*'aboda*) in verses 13-14, contrasting what is their bitter fate in Egypt with the standard use of *'abad* for serving God. Although the tide has temporarily turned against them, the entire scene opens in verse 9 with Pharaoh comparing his own people to the very formally defined "people, the children of Israel," that is, a people to be reckoned with.

C. 1:15-22: The Oppression Turns Deadly

Intensity is the keynote of section C. If forced labor will not control the divine blessing, and Israel continues to grow, then an assault on life itself can be tried. The text is filled with irony here. Slavery at least benefited the state in its building and farming projects; now they kill the very source of their labor. The midwives who represent the gift of life become the bearers of death; the Nile, which is to be the means of death, is being prepared to save the very life that will free the people. These verses continue the theme of fertility as blessing from sections A and B and prepare the way for section D and the birth of the hero. However, the outlook is desperate as Pharaoh becomes more determined. The scene ends with not just the midwives but all the Egyptians commanded to hunt down and drown Hebrew baby boys.

D. 2:1-10: The Birth of Moses

Section D has long been recognized to have affinities with the legend of the wondrous birth of Sargon of Akkad. This sets Moses' birth off as special among the thousands in the land. The direct intervention of God is nowhere mentioned, and yet the allusion to the ancient legend would have made it clear to all that this was a birth under divine protection and guidance. Ironically, Pharaoh's own daughter will be the agent of foiling his plans, and the river of death will become the vehicle of delivery for the child. In still further reversals, the boy's own mother will be able to wean him for his first years. What was to be the special fate of this child? Seven times the short story mentions "the child," echoing to the sensitive hearer that this boy will have a sevenfold greatness like the great nation of seventy that is Israel. Moses will encompass in his mission the fate of the whole people.

E. 2:11-15: *Moses Turns Deadly*

This unit is linked to the previous birth story by repeating that the child has now grown great. But there is a gap. Moses is clearly a young man. What has he thought or experienced? How much of his Hebrew heritage has he imbibed? All this can only be guessed.[7] He emerges as fully understanding and prepared for action. But in a double twist on both Israel's and his own past, he now must come to the rescue of his fellow Israelites by killing an Egyptian, fleeing the land, and becoming a sojourner in the desert — a wanderer in fear of his life as had been Jacob his ancestor. The story even ends as Jacob's flight from Esau had: sitting by a well in a foreign land (see Gen. 29:1-2).

F. 2:16-22: *Moses Becomes a Midianite*

The sixth scene in the drama finds Moses fighting once again for others who have been oppressed — this time the seven daughters of Reuel. The fate of the leader is to become a shepherd after defending the women against shepherds who had driven them off. This is still a further parallel to his ancestor Jacob in Laban's service (Gen. 30:29-43). Once settled into the role himself, he names his own son Gershom, a name that can mean both "he is a stranger here" (*ger sham*) and "he is driven out" (from the root *grsh*). In an ironic twist on his own fate, the family of Reuel takes him as an Egyptian!

G. 2:23-25: *God Recalls the Blessing*

Another gap in the story — how long does Moses stay in the land of Midian? We never find out from the text, and yet as section G rounds out the stages of waiting, God "awakens" to what is needed. Four cries of anguish in verses 23-24 are matched by four responses of God that set the

---

7. The midrashic speculations of early Jewish exegesis were very concerned to fill in the time gap that existed between the youth of Moses and his mission before Pharaoh in chapters 3 and following. This includes strong interest in the legend of how he conquered Ethiopia and ruled for forty years before returning to the land of Egypt. See Ginzberg, *The Legends of the Jews,* II: 288-91.

action of the following chapters underway: God *heard, remembered, saw,* and *knew,* all verbs that are closely tied to Israel's covenant relationship with God throughout the Hebrew Scriptures.[8]

Chiastic Structure in Exodus

The drama moves swiftly through chapters 1–2 by means of these seven vignettes where the predominant note seems to be the constant changes in people's status. Success gives way to danger, stability to precarious fate. Clearly a long time passes, the text tells us, but the rapidity with which situations change almost takes the reader's breath away. Of course, this effect is not created accidentally, for the writers have it carefully under control, and we can get a hint of their purpose when we note the effort to summarize the connection of these events to the world of the ancestral stories in Genesis: section A (1:1-7) opens this passage with a careful tabulation of the promises made beforehand (Gen. 12:1-3; 15:13-14; 35:11-12; 46:8-27) and the passage closes with section G (2:23-25) when God calls them again to mind.

Thus these seven linked stories provide a transition from Genesis as a prologue to the establishment of God's people and its accomplishment by rescue and covenant in the rest of Exodus: a theme that is made explicit in the encounter between God and Moses in Exodus 3:6-9 and 6:2-9. The incidents of Exodus 1–2 hinge on a double reversal of fate theme, that of the people and that of Moses, but by the final scene the stage will be set for a rescue that will create and seal the unity of a people and their God forever.

The seven scenes reinforce this point of dramatic reversal by means of a conscious chiastic ordering so that three incidents lead to the crucial, central panel in 2:1-10, and three lead away from it:

8. For a full discussion, see Childs, *The Book of Exodus,* 28-33.

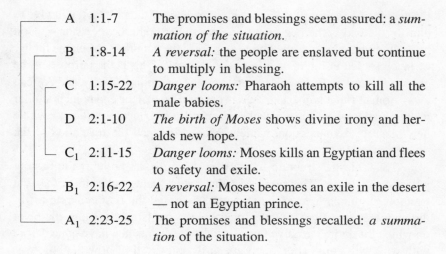

A   1:1-7   The promises and blessings seem assured: a *summation of the situation.*

B   1:8-14   A *reversal:* the people are enslaved but continue to multiply in blessing.

C   1:15-22   *Danger looms:* Pharaoh attempts to kill all the male babies.

D   2:1-10   *The birth of Moses* shows divine irony and heralds new hope.

C_1 2:11-15   *Danger looms:* Moses kills an Egyptian and flees to safety and exile.

B_1 2:16-22   A *reversal:* Moses becomes an exile in the desert — not an Egyptian prince.

A_1 2:23-25   The promises and blessings recalled: *a summation* of the situation.

A summation of Israel's success, followed by a reversal of fate into slavery, leads to great danger. That, in turn, sets the stage for the birth that will trigger the reverse direction. The rescue of the baby defeats the original danger but engenders a new danger. When he grows up, by reconnecting to Israel, Moses is forced into exile, a reversal of his privileged position; and the final summation links his helplessness to that of his people but with a promise of blessing like that of Joseph in section A. In the process of moving from blessing in section A to curse in section A_1, the turning point has already been set in place.

The chiastic structure serves to emphasize both the mirror-like quality of the action in the overall story and the irony factors. At first, everything seems to be the fulfillment of the promises to the ancestors beyond their wildest dreams: Egypt itself is their land of settlement and blessing. But in an instant their fortunes change — their very success becomes their downfall, and instead of honor as descendants of Joseph they become slaves. The situation intensifies — now oppression gives way to murder. The promise of sons so prominent in Genesis is directly attacked by Pharaoh's orders to destroy all boys. At this stage the Israelites are in dire straits. Suddenly again, in an ironic twist, the deliverance of one boy ends up making him a prince of Egypt. Now the one to be killed lives under the protection of, and even under the very eyes of, the killer. But the irony does not end there. This miraculous savior must first himself be turned on end. In a flash he is brought down from his place of honor and becomes an exile and refugee in a foreign land. In this way, Moses mirrors the fate of his people. But by becoming a microcosm of the people of Israel itself, Moses is now readied for the task God will give to him. In the end is the beginning, to reverse a common expression — God brings to mind what was the divine plan from the beginning when the family of Jacob settled in Egypt as if in a foreign world. This is the purpose of the chiasm pattern: A, B, and C lead up to the turning point; C_1, B_1, and A_1 lead away from it. But it is also like a circle or spiral, so that the end point is similar to the situation of hope in which it began in chapter 1 but now initiates a whole new plane of divine action, namely, Moses' call and the revelation of the divine name in chapter 3.

This chiastic structure focuses on the birth narrative as the turning point of the drama. The wonder of that event stands out both as the first triumph of human love in the midst of terror and the first concrete act of divine mercy that signals God's intention to save Israel. It is also the pivot on which the entire narrative turns. It links the events that have gone before with what will come after. Sections A, B, and C tell of how the Nile was to be the means of Israel's destruction, but in the birth story of D it becomes the means of salvation; Pharaoh's evil designs of murder in the first three sections are now thwarted by his own daughter's plan. In a very similar way the future is also foreshadowed. In the event of 2:1-10, a nobody becomes a prince, and the text tells us he grows great (Exod. 2:10). Ironically, in the following sections, E, F, and G, when he does grow up his situation deteriorates badly and he who was a prince now becomes a nobody again, a refugee or wanderer in the desert. What had been the promising life of a prince became a life rejected by both families, Egyptian and Hebrew alike. One further point might also be noted that turns out to be ironic: in the birth episode, Pharaoh's daughter spies the baby and it becomes a life-saving look; in the following events, the Hebrews spy on Moses' killing of the Egyptian and it becomes a life-threatening look.

Needless to say, all these twists and turns suggest to the reader that higher power and a higher purpose are governing all these events. We wait and wonder what it will all mean.

Exodus 2:1-10 and the Sargon Legend

In interpreting the central role of the birth story for the plot line of chapters 1–2, we cannot escape the significant similarities between this account of a baby set adrift by his parents and rescued by a princess to become a leader of his people and the well-known Babylonian story of the birth and adventures of King Sargon of Akkad.[9] The latter text is broken and incomplete, but the extant part contains fifty-four lines in two columns of which only the first half is really coherent enough to interpret. In the most recent in-depth study by Brian Lewis, the important opening thirteen lines are rendered:

1 Sargon, strong king, king of Agade, am I.
2 My mother was a high priestess, my father I do not know.
3 My paternal kin inhabit the mountain region.
4 My city (of birth) is Azupiranu, which lies on the bank of the Euphrates.
5 My mother, a high priestess, conceived me, in secret she bore me.
6 She placed me in a reed basket, with bitumen she caulked my hatch.
7 She abandoned me to the river from which I could not escape.
8 The river carried me along; to Aqqi, the water drawer, it brought me.
9 Aqqi, the water drawer, when immersing his bucket lifted me up.
10 Aqqi, the water drawer, raised me as his adopted son.
11 Aqqi, the water drawer, set me to his garden work.
12 During my garden work, Ishtar loved me (so that)
13 Fifty-five years I ruled as king.[10]

Without falling into an attempt to make this legend parallel to Moses' birth story in every detail, we can start with the observation that both have a similar theological theme: a child is set adrift and so put into the care of the gods to save. Where he could have been simply exposed to wild animals to be devoured quickly, care is taken to give him a chance to live if the gods so desire it. Divine providence and a period of service in a foreign place eventually lead the young hero back to his homeland and leadership.

Lewis traces the basic story to a widespread type of folktale, the "Exposed-Hero" type.[11] Lewis traces seventy-two examples through the

9. The Sargon Legend text cannot be dated exactly. Our extant example falls between 2050 and 650 B.C.E., and purports to be an autobiographical account of the life of the great founder of the first dynasty of Akkad, which overthrew the Sumerian hegemony in the twenty-fourth century.

10. The most complete study of the Sargon Legend to date is Brian Lewis, *The Sargon Legend,* ASOR Dissertation Series 4 (Cambridge, Mass.: ASOR, 1980). The text is transliterated and translated with notes on pp. 24-29. See detailed parallels to the Exodus 2 account on pp. 263-66.

11. See Lewis, *The Sargon Legend,* 211-16; 245-66.

centuries, but an exhaustive comparison reveals that only two stand close to one another: the Sargon legend and Exodus 2. They represent a basic seven-part sequence:

(1) the explanation of the coming abandonment;
(2) the noble status of the infant;
(3) preparations for exposure;
(4) exposure;
(5) special care and protection of the child;
(6) discovery and adoption;
(7) the hero grows up to do great accomplishments.

One element in this list may not seem to fit Moses' story as we have it, namely the noble status of the child. However, scholars generally understand that the Sargon story's reference to the mother as a "high priestess" can be paralleled by the Hebrew tradition that Moses' parents were both from levitical priestly families.[12]

Despite the many similarities, we must not forget that the stories are not entirely the same. The Sargon legend tells of a war leader who conquered an empire with the help of the goddess, while Moses was primarily a religious leader who led his people out of a desperate situation. On the other hand, Israelite storytellers did see two important parallels that could be emphasized by imitating the legend of mighty Sargon. Like Sargon, Moses was specially blessed by God and guided on a mission to lead his people to a new land; and at the same time he brought about a new kind of empire by replacing the deadly rule of Pharaoh by the kingdom of God. In this way, the birth story in Exodus borrows a legend in order to point ahead to the all-important mission of Moses in his later life.[13]

12. See further discussion in Sarna, *Exploring Exodus,* 30-31; B. Childs, "The Birth of Moses," *JBL* 84 (1965): 113-14; and in Lewis, *The Sargon Legend,* 265-66.

13. At the same time, many aspects of the biblical narrative are *not* found in the Sargon story: the involved development of the genocide plans of Pharaoh; the three months of being nursed and hidden at home; the role of the sister to keep the baby within the Hebrew people by a stratagem; the nursing of his own mother. Nor does the Sargon legend emphasize irony factors as strongly as the biblical version as, e.g., Pharaoh's own daughter thwarts Pharaoh's plan; the mother who abandoned the child ends up with the child anyhow.

Plot Unity and Plot Message

Although many scholars have pointed to the indications of earlier sources behind chapters 1–2,[14] there is enough literary structure to suggest a unified writing of these two chapters. The plot is developed with ever greater intensity, first against the whole people and their blessing and then, in turn, against the hero Moses and his blessing. Moreover, as several scholars have pointed out,[15] the story line keeps God in the background — divine presence and power is apparently guiding events, but not until the very final lines is God's intervention mentioned. In this way, the materials of Exodus 1–2 are similar to the Joseph story in Genesis 37–50; they seem to be the product of a school-of-wisdom writers who have crafted older material into a single unit. The power of these chapters is increased by the ominous note that lies hidden behind the text. It is not just Egyptians against Israelites; a contest is developing between Pharaoh's will to control history and the promises of Israel's God. This contest will dominate the story of the plagues and the crossing of the sea. Such pretensions to divine status are not explicitly mentioned in the Exodus text but are well-remembered later in the tradition as, for example, in Ezekiel 29:1-3; 31:1-15; 32:1-3. Since references to the divine status of Pharaoh were common in Egyptian literature, Israel would have been well-aware of them throughout her history.[16]

The reader perceives that a larger drama is being played out because of the constant ironies and reversals in the plot. One small example that hints to a life and death struggle between the gods of two peoples is the ironical development that midwives who are to bring forth life are commanded to take it but, in fact, save it. The means assigned to take life, the

14. A typical breakdown is 1:1-5, 7, 13-14; 2:23*b*-25 = P; 1:8-12; 2:15-23*a* = J; 1:15-22; 2:1-14 = E. See James Plastaras, *The God of Exodus* (Milwaukee: Collegeville, Minn.: Liturgical Press, 1962), center chart. J. Philip Hyatt, *Exodus,* provides a full listing of sources on pp. 48-49. Childs, *The Book of Exodus,* 10-11, suggests that J and P were already fused in the narrative of chapter 1 before it was joined to chapter 2.

15. See Brevard Childs, "The Birth of Moses," *JBL* 84 (1965): 109-22; Nahum Sarna, *Exodus,* 8.

16. An instructive example of this is the well-known "Hymn to the Aton" in James Pritchard, ed., *Ancient Near Eastern Texts Relating to the Old Testament,* 3rd ed. (Princeton, N.J.: Princeton Univ. Press, 1969): 369-71, which begins with a solemn identification of Pharaoh and the Aton and has been widely identified as a model for Psalm 104 in the Hebrew prayerbook.

Nile, becomes the means to save it (a further irony in that the Egyptians praised the life-giving Nile).[17] Still further, Moses' taking of a life becomes the occasion to rescue his own. Not accidentally, the second time Moses experiences a positive refuge of safety also comes at a source of water, Reuel's well. Such reversals involving water will culminate later in the book at the great moment at the Reed Sea.

In all of these dramatic turns, a two-step action occurs. The first step is always secret or private, followed by a public step: (1) Pharaoh plots; then orders enslavement. (2) Pharaoh instructs the midwives; then they go forth to thwart his plan. (3) The baby is hidden; then found and brought up a prince. (4) Moses' killing is secret; but when revealed it causes him to flee. (5) The private action at the well for a small group leads to his public inclusion in a new tribal family. The effect of such consistent two-step action is to create a sense of wonderment and puzzlement about what will happen next. Outcomes are not certain at first, and the result often surprises the reader. It reinforces the unspoken realization that a greater and more mysterious drama is unfolding than any single incident reveals.

Genesis as Prologue

The drama in Exodus 1–2 is more than a setting for the great acts of liberation that follow in chapters 3–15. It bridges the whole mysterious past of promises found in Genesis and the drama of the coming Exodus. In fact, it surely presupposes that the reader knows Genesis from beginning to end, since it develops in depth four crucial themes found there: (1) the primeval blessing to all peoples (Gen. 1:28; 5:2; 9:1); (2) the flood story of Genesis 6–9 in which the righteous family is saved but the wicked drown; (3) the promises of land and progeny in Genesis 12:1-3 and other passages; (4) the story of Joseph whose wisdom saved Egypt and brought his family prosperity.

In (1) Pharaoh tried to harness the Nile waters like the chaos waters of Genesis 1:2 to destroy Israel, but God's blessing continues on the people; in (2) the ark in which Moses is hidden is called a *teba,* a word used elsewhere only of Noah's ark (twenty-five times in Genesis 6–9!).[18] It

---

17. See, e.g., the "Hymn to the Nile," in Pritchard, *Ancient Near Eastern Texts,* 372-73.

18. Because the word for Moses' little basket is the same as for the ark that saved

reinforces the reference to blessing in Genesis 1 since the Nile will not become another flood to destroy God's people. In (3) there are many verbal connections to the promises of Genesis 28:14-15; 35:11-12; 46:8-27 (= Exod. 1:1-7), but above all, the reader recalls the fundamental promise of God's first word to Abraham: "I will bless those who bless you, and the one who curses you I will curse" (Gen. 12:3) — the reversal of fate that will bring Israel out on top will bring Egypt down. Finally in (4) the wisdom motifs of the Joseph story play a role. As Joseph was betrayed by his brothers yet delivered them in time of famine, so Moses, despite being betrayed by his own, would deliver them.

This leads us to our final note on the interaction of plot and message. In the larger plot of the books of Genesis and Exodus, our seven parts of Exodus 1–2 form a unified turning point that is sandwiched between the promises to the ancestors and their real completion under Moses:

Genesis 12–50   The promises are given but fulfilled only partially and wrongly, in Egypt!

Exodus 1–2   Transition and reversal of situation.

Exodus 3–15   The promises find a new direction of fulfillment as the people leave Egypt.

Ramifications for Preachers

This does not exhaust the analysis of these passages in Exodus 1–2. The standard commentaries point to many instances of irony and suggestive themes beyond the few remarks here. I have been more interested in awakening in the reader a sense of the purposive literary structure that not only provides some historical background and numerous theological motifs that will be developed in the further story of the Exodus (as well as in the

---

the whole human race, it seems clear that the authors of Exodus 2 want us to see Moses as a savior of his people very much in the image of Noah who saved all peoples. It is also worth noting that the Sargon legend describes the reed basket in terms very similar to the description of Noah's ark in Genesis 6. The Moses story is also very close to some elements of the Mesopotamian version of the flood in the Gilgamesh Epic in which the ark that rescued Utnapishtim and his family from the flood was also of reed like Sargon's basket. This verbal tie links all four stories: the Gilgamesh flood story, Noah's ark, the Sargon legend, and Moses' birth.

prophetic reflections on loyalty to Israel's God alone) but will also help us realize that both Christian and Jewish readers can share the same understanding of the text. Its literary shape is not *all* that the text has to say to our two faiths, but it does give us both a mutual obediential reverence for the God whom we both acknowledge as ruler and guider of the universe and as savior of the chosen people whose story we have both accepted as our story.

In preparing a sermon on Exodus 1–2, or on the birth story in Exodus 2:1-10 only, the preacher should bring out the dramatic turns in the plot as signs of the mysterious ways of God. No one should preach on these verses without showing them to be the first stage of the great act of liberation that will take place in the following chapters. They sound the central themes of both God's will to save no matter what we might do and God's ability to turn the evil of human designs to the good. A second value of exploring for the congregation the dramatic moments in the plot is to point out how the biblical writers were so conscious that God actually works through the ups and downs of human actions in history. God uses our situations to show us how to find God in our midst. The stories of Exodus challenge all hearers of the word to find the hand of God in the world and more particularly in the situations of their own lives. Further, the ironical reversals are included in the narratives precisely to remind all of us in subsequent ages that God does have a plan that weaves its way through human events, sometimes hidden, sometimes seemingly obvious, but never so clear and simple that we can control it to turn it to our advantage or to thwart it by our actions. In this same vein, the text invites the preacher to reflect on the issue of prayer in dark moments. These passages tell us that God always hears and answers prayer but not always in the way we think best or according to our timetables.

Many of the central themes of these first two chapters of Exodus have particular significance for Christian preachers. Although they have not been selected to appear in the common Sunday lectionary at all, a regrettable omission from my point of view, they make wonderful texts to preach on over several days in a row.[19] It is a story of God's exaltation of

---

19. Although Exodus 1–2 do not appear as lectionary readings for the triennial cycle, the next passage in Exodus 3 — the call of Moses at the burning bush — occurs on the third Sunday of Lent in cycle C and might make an opportune occasion to context the call in the preceding events. These chapters are suggested, however, for daily use in the fifteenth week of the year in Catholic lectionaries.

Moses after his humiliation and rejection; it is a divine plan worked from suffering to victory; and it illustrates that sometimes God works in mysterious ways, especially counter to human expectations, in order to be revealed to us. St. Matthew already draws out many of these thoughts in his prologue to his Gospel in Matthew 1–2, the birth story of Jesus, a story partially modeled after Exodus 1–2 (see note 3). But we can also note the theme of divine wisdom that in Exodus echoes the Joseph story of Genesis; it is found in Paul's reflections on how divine wisdom can be discovered in what others would consider the folly of the cross (1 Cor. 2–4).

To use these texts effectively in Christian preaching, however, we must treat Exodus not as a prediction of Christ's coming but as a parallel event. Moses and Jesus both illustrate the wondrous working of divine grace that confounds human evil and upends human expectations while issuing forth in a deeper and more profound insight into divine governance of the world and divine compassion and love for human beings.

The Burning Bush
through the Eyes of Midrash:
God's Word Then and Now

A. STANLEY DREYFUS

*"No place is devoid of God's presence, not even a
thornbush." (Exodus Rabbah 2:5)*

Midrash is a term that comes from a Hebrew root meaning "to search" or
"to investigate." It is a classic Jewish mode of Bible study and is built
upon the conviction that Scripture, as Leo Baeck wrote,

> did not only tell something, it also meant something. . . . It was much
> more than a mere book. . . . Hence it was also quite insufficient merely
> to read and to know it; it had to be discovered again and again, word
> for word. . . . The word one read could never be a merely written and
> fixed word: it always spoke, moved, and progressed. It always had
> something new to say. . . .[1]

The various collections of Midrash, some of which will be cited in
these pages, constitute a literature replete with exuberant imagery, extrav-
agant fantasies, stories, parables, exotic folklore, and tantalizing obscuri-

1. Leo Baeck, *Judaism and Christianity* (Philadelphia, 1958): 46, 50.

ties. Yet, they addressed themselves to timeless and universal concerns, and, because human nature is remarkably constant, the questions put two millennia ago are very often replicated by the questing minds of our day.

We begin with several midrashic perceptions that are built upon Hebrew wordplays. The "Mountain of God" is named Horeb (Exodus 3:1). The *h* of *Horeb* is really the guttural *ch* familiar to those who speak German. In Hebrew the vowels are represented by points above, beneath, or along-side the consonants. Only the consonants were inscribed in the old texts of Scripture; the vowels were added, in accordance with a tradition of how the words were to be pronounced, by the Masorites as recently as the seventh century C.E. Vowels are included in the printed texts of the Hebrew Bible but not in the manuscript scrolls that are read in the synagogue. The absence of vowels in the manuscripts allows the consonants of *Horeb* to be read *herev*, "sword," which to the rabbis implied that the revelation of Horeb-Sinai, if neglected or disobeyed, would lead inevitably to the sword, to strife and destruction (Exodus Rabba 2:4). Furthermore, if the second and third consonants of *Horeb* are reversed, the word becomes *haber,* "friend" and in a broader sense "friendship" or "society." This fancy suggested that if a society is to endure, it must be founded upon an alliance, upon the closest association with the One who made himself and his will known at Horeb (cf. *Midrash Lekah Toy, Shemot* 3:2).

Again, the noun *seneh*, "bush," shares two consonants with *Sinai,* and in pronunciation the words can easily be taken each for the other. Close to these in sound, though with a different final consonant, is the root *sanei',* "to hate." The Midrash recognizes that Jews' stubborn adherence to the Law of Sinai sets them apart from others and often gives rise to *sinei',* to hatred against Israel (Exodus Rabba 2:6). Here is an ancient explanation for preju-dice. All too many human beings find it strangely difficult to tolerate those who differ from them in the color of their skin, the shape of their eyes, in their way of life, their values, their accent. Antipathies persist for no valid reason; baseless hatreds proliferate. When will we learn to love all God's children? When will *sinei'* be eradicated by the teachings of Sinai?

*   *   *

"Now Moses was keeping the flock of Jethro . . ." (Exod. 3:1)

According to the Midrash, God tests the character of those who aspire to leadership by entrusting them with responsibility for a flock of sheep. So

God did with David, with Amos, with Moses. Moses watched over Jethro's flock so devotedly that he proved his worthiness to be Israel's shepherd through the desert wanderings. Once upon a time, say the rabbis, a lamb darted away from the herd, pausing only to gulp water from each brooklet. Finally Moses overtook it. "Poor lamb, I did not realize how parched you were. Surely now you are tired." So saying, he raised the creature to his shoulder and carried it back to the flock. Then God spoke: "Because you have taken pity on the lamb, you shall pasture my people Israel" (Yalkut on Exod. 3:1).

The old metaphor that likens God's people to mindless sheep that are totally dependent upon their pastors for protection and sustenance no longer reflects the image most men and women hold of themselves and their place in church and synagogue. In the current vocabulary of religion the clergy are perceived as facilitators, as those who empower their people. Most of our members (or potential members) decline to accept rabbis, priests, and ministers in the shepherd's traditional role, doling out fodder, corralling the flock to keep out interlopers, deciding where the sheep may be allowed to graze. Nonetheless, many continue to look to us to watch over them, to relieve their hunger, to find them shelter against the cold. The mentally ill who drift vacantly and aimlessly along our streets need us, as do the unemployed who have been stripped of their security and their dignity, as do the battered wives, and the neglected and abused children, as do those too infirm or too poor to supply their own wants, as do the disease-ridden, waiting for the final release and dreading it. All these require more than palliatives. Our shepherd's task remains perennially valid: to make ourselves proactive; to constitute ourselves God's impatient coworkers, shepherds that tend the flocks of the hapless and helpless. Only so do we demonstrate ourselves fit for the vocation to which we believe ourselves called.

Yet, the metaphor retains something of its early impact, because even the healthy and the worldly successful seek us out to be their shepherds. They crave to be led by men and women of faith and uprightness. They yearn to be reassured that God lives and loves, that we humans have power from God to renew justice and to establish a society in which peace will be at home. When our deeds are unfailingly consistent with what we profess, even the most independent and self-reliant may be induced to accept our guidance and to walk with us in holy pilgrimage. On our text the Zohar remarks:

The Holy One, blessed be He, foresaw that Moses would shepherd Israel as he shepherded Jethro's flock, the males as they required, and the females likewise, according to their needs. (Zohar, *Shemot,* 21a)

The Midrash elaborates:

Moses would loose the smaller animals first, allowing them to graze upon the tender grass. Then he led out the older sheep to feed upon the ordinary vegetation, and finally he released the fully-grown sheep so that they could pasture on the hard stubble that was left over, pabulum adequate to their needs, yet indigestible by the other animals. Said God: "Let the one who knows how to feed the flock, each according to its needs, now come to feed My people." (Exodus Rabba 2:2)

Lawrence A. Hoffman and Nancy Wiener have recast this parable into a timely reminder that we clergy must acknowledge and allow for the substantial differences that exist among our people. They call us to:

a recognition that not all our worshippers are the same, a sense that the liturgy must not exclude anyone. Our congregations are filled with women and men, children and adults, young and old, sick and well. There are married and unmarried; people with family needs and individuals seeking private consolation or spiritual purpose. There are homosexuals and lesbians, single parent families, people without children (of necessity or by design), converts to Judaism, the Jewishly educated and the Jewishly naive.[2]

Mutatis mutandis, we do indeed minister to many disparate congregations within our single congregation, and each constituent of these separate congregations, according to his or her understanding, and often in terms of his or her desperation, is reaching out to us as clergy, hungry for our own insights as well as for the official teachings of the religious body for which we are authorized to speak. Some will be easily satisfied. Others will be disappointed at our advice, dismissing it as irrelevant and ourselves as outmoded. They may grow increasingly strident in assailing us when we cannot agree with their opinions, when we cannot affirm the wisdom

2. Lawrence A. Hoffman and Nancy Wiener, "The Liturgical State of the World Union for Progressive Judaism," *European Judaism* 6 (1991): 17.

of the course they want to pursue. Yet, each of them, however obstreperous, is worthy of our time, our empathy, our prayers, and whatever material assistance we can provide.

So we are needed, as shepherds, as teachers of time-tried morality, as facilitators, as enablers, as role models, but we are needed to carry on our special ministry of listening, of reconciling, of healing, of caring, of loving people for themselves, for their virtues and their faults, for their unity and their diversity.

In a discussion of diversity, one issue calls for special emphasis. The passage we quoted from the Zohar describes Moses' awareness of the distinctive needs of males and females in the flock. Hundreds of books and articles have been written in recent years to document the discrimination women have had to endure throughout history. Despite the widespread attention that this evil has received, it persists, little diminished.

Sensitive authors, both men and women, have tried to sensitize us to the unhappy fate imposed upon half the human race. Helen Pearson shares her feelings with quiet dignity and persuasive sincerity:

As an Adventist woman, I am aware that there is one time more than any other, and one place more than any other, that my needs are not addressed and my experience not utilized because I am a woman. The time: Sabbath morning. The place: the church service. . . . As far as leadership in worship is concerned, there is no one who is "like" me. No one relating to God from a woman's perspective. No one who has come through childhood hearing and believing that God is "He" and therefore more like her father and her brother than like herself and her mother.[3]

*   *   *

". . . and he led the flock to the farthest end
of the wilderness . . ." (Exod. 3:1)

The Sages regarded the wilderness as a no-man's-land. Because no one claimed ownership of it, every shepherd was free to graze his flock there. Its vegetation was free for the taking. Into the most remote reaches of this

3. Helen Pearson, "All Things to All [Wo]men," *Ministry* (Journal of the Seventh-Day Adventist Ministerial Association), January 1992, 14ff.

wilderness Moses led Jethro's sheep, for fear that the animals, though carefully guarded, might somehow stray and strip fields for which others had paid dearly in order to pasture their own herds, fields that were close to their own houses, and thus especially convenient for the shepherds. Moses thrust aside any advantage for himself, so that he might avoid becoming an unintentional predator, stealing what others had toiled to accumulate (*Yalkut* on Exod. 3:1).

This exquisite sensitivity to the rights of private property, which the rabbis read back into the beginnings of Israel's history, has become noticeably impaired nowadays. Our age is blighted by crime on a grand scale in the marketplace, by allegations of wrongdoing on every level of government, and most recently by the hijacking of automobiles at gunpoint, and by the comparatively petty thefts of children who snatch jewelry, jackets, bicycles from their classmates. "Cheating is everywhere," declares the author of a new handbook on the most effective ways of applying the technique so as to earn high grades in university examinations (*New York Times,* Dec. 26, 1991). The malefactors, though they seldom regard themselves in that light, too often grow up to become our politicians, our repairpeople, our financiers, even our researchers. The rabbis, searching for explanations to account for the fall of Jerusalem, God's chosen city and the site of the Temple, maintained that one of the chief causes of the tragedy had to be widespread dishonesty in business transactions (*Babylonian Talmud, Shabbat* 119b).

The rabbis offered a second reason to justify God's having allowed Jerusalem to fall: that people no longer reproved each other for their misdeeds. Corruption thus took on the veneer of respectability, and miscreants were elevated to positions of honor and trust. What standards of behavior are we to expect of those who are considered for leadership in our congregations? No human being is without fault, and none of us wants to be stigmatized as a promoter of controversy, but when principle and prudence clash, on which side shall the clergy be found? Here is an excruciating dilemma that few of us can avoid in the course of our ministry. Another relevant concern for us:

The Sages, looking into the shepherd's heart, discerned that some shepherds fell into the habit of granting themselves dispensations. They would say: I do not steal for my own advantage, but for the need of those creatures that depend upon me for their sustenance. Since I have nothing of my own with which to feed them, and since the Torah forbids that they be abandoned to suffer hunger, society is responsible for their care. So the shepherd allows himself to pasture the flock in fields that are another's property. On the basis of such faulty reasoning, the gullible do not hesitate to disregard the commandment against theft, although, "Thou shalt not steal," (Exodus 20:13) forbids you to take property which belongs to someone else, whether for your own advantage, or for the advantage of others. You may not take it to satisfy your own needs, nor anybody else's.[4]

*   *   *

*"... and he led the flock to the farthest end
of the wilderness ..." (Exod. 3:1)*

In the religious consciousness of Israel their sojourn in the wilderness remained determinative ever after. Whenever the people, seduced by the material and the expedient, abandoned the truths they had gleaned through their desert wanderings, Hosea and Jeremiah, the prophets of the wilderness, called them back to the austerity of the desert (Hos. 2:14-15; Jer. 2:2-3). Edmond Fleg comments:

> The faithful shepherd, in order to pasture Jethro's flock, went day by day deeper into the wilderness; a compulsion drew him thither: he sought the presence of God. If one would have an immediate experience of God, he must first create a wilderness within himself.[5]

A wilderness within the soul. Setting up one's very own inner enclave, freely chosen silence, solitude wherein to reflect undisturbed upon God and created things, to contemplate erstwhile wonders that through familiarity are no longer wonders, merely commonplace and tedious. In that detached life of solitude and contemplation, the commonplace is once again imbued with mystery.

Rabbi Abraham Yaakov of Sadagora told his disciples:

> "What man has made has something to teach us."
> "What can we learn from a train?" asked one.
> "That because of a single second one can miss everything."

---

4. *Tal Mishpat,* quoted in Aaron J. Greenberg, *Itturei Torah* (Tel Aviv, 1970): 3, 27.
5. Edmond Fleg, *Moses* (Munich, n.d.): 26f.

"And from the telegraph?"
"That every word is counted and charged."
"And the telephone?"
"That what we say here is heard there."[6]

What lessons would Abraham Yaakov have drawn out of today's technology? What truths would he have seen in the computer, in the spaceship, in the laser beam, in the genetic code?

Nor is it ever too late to create the wilderness within ourselves.

Days pass and the years vanish, and we walk sightless among miracles. Lord, fill our eyes with seeing and our minds with knowing; let there be moments when Your Presence, like lightning, illumines the darkness in which we walk. Help us to see, wherever we gaze, that the bush burns unconsumed. And we, clay touched by God, will reach out for holiness and exclaim in wonder: How filled with awe is this place, and we did not know it! Blessed is the Eternal One, the holy God![7]

*   *   *

". . . and he came to the mountain of God." (Exodus 3:1)

As Moses neared Horeb, it seemed merely another mountain with nothing striking about it. What reason did Scripture have for styling it in advance "the mountain of God," a distinction it did not yet merit? The Midrash declares that the name is given "with respect to the future" (*Sifrei* Deuteronomy, Ch. 22). It is an anticipatory declaration. When the bush will have ignited, and the angel of the Lord will have appeared out of the flame, then the height will have earned its name, "the mountain of God."

So in our lives. We cannot anticipate the future of a casual encounter with a stranger. A simple introduction and its conventional acknowledgment may initiate a lifelong friendship. A word may point the way to a career or bring about a radical transformation. *Tolle, lege,* "Take up, read," a child sang at play, and a heedless young man overheard, and pondered, and discovered a deeper significance in the syllables. History remembers him

6. Martin Buber, *Tales of the Hasidim,* 2 (New York, 1948): 70.
7. *Gates of Prayer: The New Union Prayerbook* (New York, 1975): 170f.

as St. Augustine.[8] According to the Talmud, Simeon ben Lakish had extraordinary strength of body. To earn his livelihood he abandoned the study of the Law and became a *ludarius,* a circus performer who wrestled with wild animals. One day, chancing by, Rabbi Jochanan said, "Your strength would be better devoted to Torah." That was all. Simeon left the ring, resumed his studies, and won renown as scholar and teacher, yet up to that time he had been known only as a gladiator. Ben Azzai was in the habit of saying: "Despise not any person, and do not reject anything, for there is not a person that has not his or her hour, and there is not a thing that has not its place" (*Babylonian Talmud, Gittin* 47a, *Baba Metsia'* 84a; *Mishnah Abot* 4:3). We should hesitate to fault the one who has not yet discovered his or her place in life. There may yet be a glorious future in store for such a one. We are not told in advance which insignificant elevation will be forever after known as "the mountain of God."

*   *   *

"And the angel of the Lord appeared to him in a flame
of fire out of the midst of a bush . . ." (Exod. 3:2)

According to the Midrash, a heathen once asked Rabbi Joshua ben Karchah: "Why did God choose a thorn-bush from which to speak to Moses?" Joshua replied: "Had it been a carob tree or a sycamore tree, you would have asked the same question. Still, it is not right to dismiss you unanswered. It is intended to teach you that no place is devoid of God's presence, not even a thorn-bush" (Exodus Rabba 2:5). Another Rabbi observed that in the case of a human being, the bush would be an intolerable dwelling place: the sharp thorns would lacerate the flesh beyond endurance. Yet, God, in selecting a location that would cause men or women exquisite physical torment, is symbolically affirming that God unites with the Hebrews in their anguish, that their pain is God's as well. So Isaiah affirms: "In all their affliction He was afflicted" (Isa. 63:9). Likewise, speaking in God's name, the psalmist declares: "I will be with them in trouble" (Ps. 91:15). The Midrash elaborates:

> The Hebrews suffer by reason of their slavery. I reveal Myself out of the bush, out of a restricted place, all nettles and briers, in order to show

8. *Confessions of St. Augustine,* trans. Max Warner (New York, 1963): 8.12, 182.

you, so to say, that I experience *my children's torment* as if it were *my very own.* (Exodus Rabba, 2:5)

God suffers with his children. Yet, why does an omnipotent God allow them to suffer? Henry Slonimsky finds an answer to the Midrash:

> Throughout the Midrash there is implied a God-concept which is profoundly at variance with that of the philosophers and with that of the official pronouncements of the Synagogue. That God of the Midrash is not an infinite God; he is not omnipotent. He is one among many powers; he is the power for good, among the other, indifferent and dark, forces of the universe, among which, and most heartbreaking of all, is human perversity and human stupidity. . . . God can forgive, but the silly omnipotence which can play fast and loose with the laws of truth and morality, or which can pretend to undo the effects of evil once these have been launched upon the world, is denied him.[9]

The Midrash — as Slonimsky interprets it — makes it easier for us to accept the silence of God amid the enormities of the Holocaust and the other atrocities that humans, rejecting their humanity, inflict upon each other. The God who is infinite Love yet who cannot intervene to deliver his loved ones is the God we can understand out of our own love and powerlessness — and to whom we have to pledge our feeble strength.

*   *   *

"And when the Lord saw that he turned aside to see, God called unto him . . ." (Exod. 3:4)

God had already begun to speak, says the Midrash, yet Moses was so intent upon his shepherd's duties that he did not hear. For that reason God created the miracle of the bush in order to attract Moses' attention. Even then, he merely looked up and turned his head. For all his curiosity at seeing the enigma of the bush enveloped in flames that failed to devour it, Moses persisted in carrying on his work. Well satisfied with this evidence of

---

9. Henry Slonimsky, *Essays* (Cincinnati: Hebrew Union College Press, 1967): 7ff. A similar analysis of the problem is given by E. S. Brightman, *A Philosophy of Religion* (New York, 1940): 313ff.

Moses' fidelity to the task he had accepted, God declared: "This man is worthy to lead Israel" (Exodus Rabba 2:6).

The single-mindedness depicted here evokes our admiration, but any activity carried to excess runs the danger of becoming pernicious. All of us know clergy who give themselves to the routine obligations of their ministry with the most remarkable dedication. They will not be distracted. Yet, that total immersion may be nothing more than a device for avoiding familial responsibilities or other and less attractive demands upon their time and their energy. All of us will affirm the need for constant study. In order to carry on a ministry effectively, especially in an age in which many of our people are university graduates, we are compelled to keep ourselves abreast of the latest scientific theories, with new concepts in political and social science, certainly with current contributions to theology. All these need interpretation in light of the classic teachings of faith. Surely we must gain some familiarity with the universe of discourse of all classes of our people if we are to attract them and to retain them. No one will challenge that, and, yet, because we are human, most of us have become adept at contriving plausible rationalizations for attending scrupulously to every legitimate task — except to stretch our minds, to confront the new, to evaluate it, and to assimilate it. We nod in the direction of the bush when we had better give it our fullest attention. The flocks we tend are more sentient than the sheep of the wilderness.

*   *   *

". . . put off thy shoes from off thy feet . . ." (Exod. 3:5)

Said Rabbi Ephraim Luntshitz: "The roadway is rugged, and walking is hard, though when you wear shoes, you can step lightly over small stones, almost without feeling them. But when you walk unshod, every pebble is a source of irritation. For this reason *God bade Moses, leader-to-be of Israel,* to remove his shoes. In each generation leaders must keep themselves sensitive to every obstacle in the path of their people. They must suffer with them in their mishaps, must share their discomfort and their pain."[10]

*   *   *

10. *Ollelot Ephraim,* quoted in Aaron J. Greenberg, *Itturei Torah,* op. cit.

". . . put off thy shoes from off thy feet, for the place
whereon thou standest is holy ground." (Exod. 3:5)

Several medieval commentators understood Moses' compliance with the commandment issuing from the bush to signify that in a symbolic sense he was divesting himself of all activities carried out on unhallowed ground. He was severing his connection to the earthly and the mundane in order to commence a radically different way of life, dedicated exclusively to the service of God and Israel. In that new life his concentration upon God's work required that he give up his earthly pleasures, and, therefore, to the very end of his days, Moses abstained from marital relations (*Yalkut Reuveni* on Exod. 3:5; Zohar, *Chukkat* 180a, *Pikkudei* 222a).

This is an astounding observation in view of Judaism's positive attitude toward marital sex. Yet, Moses is described as willing to give up these gratifications, physical and spiritual, for what he took to be the higher, holier mission of emancipating the Hebrew slaves, of bringing them into the covenant at Sinai, of persuading them to accept its moral restraints. The celibate Moses is not likely to influence the sexual attitudes of very many men and women of our time. Nevertheless, this snippet of exegesis — or better, eisegesis — might profitably motivate some serious reflection.

The consequences of today's sexual promiscuity are grim. Statistics released by the government show that high school students have more than one million unintended pregnancies each year and about three million cases of sexually transmitted diseases. Unmarried children are begetting children for whom the emotionally immature and financially deprived parents cannot provide even rudimentary nurturing, assuming that the father is known and is willing to share responsibility with the mother. How many babies are abandoned, abused, murdered because those upon whom this unwelcome burden has been thrust become unnerved at the wailing of their unwanted, unloved offspring? And those tough enough to survive grow up to become the latest generation of the welfare-dependent, starved for affection, deprived of the security of a family and of models from whom they can learn how to live a proper life. So they become truants and eventually dropouts, ignorant of the basic skills required to earn the most modest livelihood in our increasingly complex society. All too few of them have had even a passing introduction to church or synagogue, to the values that religion teaches.

In a well-meant effort to contain the situation, some schools have undertaken to distribute condoms and to offer instruction in their use to high school students who request them. When this innovation began in New York, a newspaper published a photograph of a boy and girl, reporting their names and quoting them to the effect that as yet they did not require the devices just issued them but no doubt they would one day. The Talmud, in the passage previously quoted, offered yet another reason for the fall of Jerusalem: that its people had lost their sense of shame.

If these unprecedented measures will save a single life from the scourge of AIDS or prevent the birth of a single unwanted infant, then perhaps they may be defensible. Yet, there must be a better way. Surely there are young people who are revolted at the wretched consequences of promiscuity and who will accept counseling and appreciate encouragement to postpone sexual activity until they have an education, until they are emotionally mature enough to marry and to give their children a fair start in life. It is for us to make them aware of the vast difference between physical gratification and a lasting love and to help them reach the understanding that they need not abandon their principles and their common sense in order to win a degree of popularity among their contemporaries.

*   *   *

When, as the Midrash has it, Moses came near the bush, God considered: "If I speak to him in My own voice, he will be numbed with fear." Thereupon God resorted to a manner of speaking which Moses knew well: God spoke to him in the tones of Moses' father Amram. Overjoyed, Moses cried out: "My father still lives!" God continued: "I am the God of thy father . . ." (*Midrash Hagadol* on Exod. 3:6).

Whether the Word sounds through the loving accents of parents, of our spouse, our children, a teacher, a friend; whether we read it on a sacred page or sense it through reflection upon our own life's experience; whether we find it in stories of ancient miracles or in the wonders of our own time; whether we are directed to it by the heroic faith of martyrs or by the steadfast courage of those who wrest triumph out of adversity, surely the burden of God's message is that Moses' work is not yet done, that it is for us to take up his mission, though reluctantly, hesitatingly, because we know our limitations. Still we must, because that is God's will for us: to rescue today's politically and economically and socially and morally oppressed, to deliver them from every form of slavery — the body from addiction, the mind from prejudice, the spirit from despair, the entire being from fear — to lead them out of bondage into covenant with the Highest. Like Moses we will not complete the work, but we will do all that is in our power. And God, to whom suffering is no stranger, will walk with us on that painful trek toward Sinai.

A Night for Crying/Weeping

WALTER BRUEGGEMANN

"The God of Israel is powerfully, actively, decisively,
violently present on the side of freedom for the exploited."

This chapter comes at the end of the plague cycle. But what a mouthful! The plague cycle concerns a highly stylized narrative featuring a series of ominous encounters between established imperial power (Pharaoh and his advisors) and the assertive power of Yahweh, voiced by the uncredentialed Moses and his brother Aaron. We reduce this series of encounters to manageable proportion by the term *cycle* in an attempt to routinize and render innocuous an odd and unsettling release of holy power in the world.

The series may be appropriated historically, liturgically, or as a series of "history-initiations," though the categories are not mutually exclusive. (a) If we appropriate the narrative historically, we may seek to "explain" what happened "naturally, without recourse to any inscrutable element.[1]

---

1. For an extreme example of an historical-scientific "explanation" of the plagues, see Greta Hort, "The Plagues of Egypt," *ZAW* 69 (1957): 84-303. See the critical comment upon her work by Brevard S. Childs, *The Book of Exodus*, OTL (Philadelphia: Westminster Press, 1974): 168. Such an attempt as that of Hort helps us very little in engaging the narrative. For a very different, suggestive interpretation of the plague narrative as theological literature, see Jürgen Kegler, "Zu Komposition und Theologie der Plagenerzählungen," *Die Hebräische Bibel und ihre zweifache Nachgeschichte*, ed. Erhard Blum et al. (Neukirchen-Vluyn: Neukirchener Verlag, 1990): 55-74.

Such an effort is futile, for any such "explanation" by definition eliminates the very subject and actor that interests the storyteller. Thus at the outset, we must forego any attempt to "explain" the narrative according to our modern canons of the possible. The narrative immediately draws us into a more dangerous, unstable world where the powerful are rendered helpless before a power that overwhelms and intimidates.

(b) The stories can be understood liturgically and likely should be taken as such. By liturgy I mean only that the repetitive pattern suggests that the stories were formed for regular telling and hearing in communities familiar with the plot line and able to anticipate each successive episode. (The repetitive pattern is not unlike such television shows as "M*A*S*H" and "Cheers" and "L.A. Law" in which the same characters do the same thing in each episode and in which each listener [viewer] can anticipate the action in each new episode.) The purpose of such ritual is not the communication of new information to the listening community, for the "information" is already fully known. It is, rather, to form and nurture the imagination of the community so that its perception and experience of the world should be through the lens of this staging of reality. Specifically, the world is enacted (and hopefully appropriated) as an *agon* (struggle) between the powerful and the oppressed in which the stakes are very high, the confrontation vigorous, and the outcome sure. In such a rendering, the decisive character, Yahweh, is easily rendered as one of the regulars in the plot. The imagination of this community thus comes to include Yahweh as a character in the normal plotting of life.

(c) To speak of this narrative as "history-initiating" appeals to the phrasing of Martin Buber, who characterized the miraculous events around the Exodus as events of "abiding astonishment."[2] The inexplicable events of liberation intend to power and energize the imagination of Israel in particular ways and to continue to impact that imagination long after the event itself is completed. The narrative asserts that at the taproot of Israel's existence is a God (mediated by Moses) who engaged with the enslaving empire and who prevailed against that empire. This history-initiating action, that is, action that makes possible a mode of public life for Israel, other

2. Martin Buber, *Moses: The Revelation and the Covenant* (Atlantic Highlands, N.J.: Humanities Press International, Inc., 1988): 75. For a commentary on Buber's suggestive phrase, see Emil Packenheim, *God's Presence in History* (New York: Harper and Row, 1972): 8-14, and Walter Brueggemann, *Abiding Astonishment: Psalms, Modernity, and the Making of History* (Louisville: Westminster/John Knox Press, 1991).

than oppression, may indeed be undertaken liturgically. Thus the liturgical
staging of these history-initiating events recruited each new generation of
Israelites into a peculiar notion of historical reality. This peculiar notion of
historical reality flies in the face of the dominant view of reality fostered
and legitimated by the powers of the empire.

What a peculiar notion of historical reality this is! The plague cycle
places the slave community (powered by Yahweh, voiced by Moses) into
deep conflict with established authority. At the center of each episode is
the assertion that Yahweh has unleashed massive, destructive power by
mobilizing the forces of creation, which are at the behest of Yahweh. On
the one hand, this unleashing is a show of power that overwhelms the
ostensive power of the empire. Thus the "plagues" establish Yahweh as
more powerful than the empire. On the other hand, this massive, seemingly
undisciplined power is in the service and interest of the slave community,
for it is that community that benefits from Yahweh's show of power.

I have noted that in chapter 11 we are at the end of the plague cycle.
The effect of the entire recital of smitings of the empire is cumulative. That
is, the persistence of God, the enactment of violence, the buoyance of the
slaves-about-to-be-freed, and the helplessness of the empire all build in
intensity and suspense. By the time we reach this final plague, the deepness
and significance of the conflict means that the suspense cannot any longer
be sustained. This confrontation will need to be the decisive act of God.
And indeed, it is.

I

The narrative of this episode begins with the initiative of God in speech
and in action (Exod. 11:1-3). The beginning point is the sovereign speech
of God addressed to Moses, consisting in a promise and a demand (Exod.
11:1-2). The promise is that Yahweh will assault Pharaoh and Egypt yet
one more time. This speech of Yahweh signals that the recital is reaching
its climax; we are now facing the decisive act. Yahweh is the sworn enemy
of Pharaoh and of Egypt. It is worth noting that throughout this chapter,
and indeed throughout the entire Exodus narrative, the critique of and
assault upon Egypt is aimed at the royal establishment. Such a focus lends
support to the view that the conflict with Egypt is not with the land of
Egypt or with the people of Egypt but only with the political, economic
power arrangements that have organized wealth to serve the few. The focus

is not unlike that of U.S. leaders who have said in the past that our quarrel is not with the "Russian people" but with the "government." The growing monopoly of goods, power, and wealth in the hands of the few in Egypt is anticipated in Genesis 47:13-26. The royal apparatus in that narrative proceeds systematically to confiscate land and wealth from other Egyptians. The process of enslavement thus is not a violent act of imposition but a process of gradual economic erosion and indebtedness.

The promise of Yahweh continues with the anticipation that Pharaoh will not only release the slaves but will vigorously dispatch them. The infinitive absolute "drive out" suggests that Pharaoh will be relieved at the departure of Israel and forcibly urge the Israelite slaves to depart. Thus Yahweh's strategy is to vex Pharaoh until the Exodus becomes a relief to the Egyptians. In the end the loss of cheap labor is worth the cost of cheap labor, for the sake of ending the vexation caused by Yahweh.

The release from debt-bondage under the Egyptians might have been enough for the slaves. Yahweh, however, will not have this people leave the empire empty-handed or without dignity. Thus the command issued by God is that upon leaving the empire, every adult slave who leaves will "ask" silver and gold from their Egyptian neighbors.[3] Two comments are evoked by this provision. First, the command is in compliance with the Israelite provision for the "year of release" (cf. Deut. 15:1-11) in which debt slaves are to be given provision in order to reenter the economy. In Deuteronomy 15:1-11 a series of five infinitive absolutes are used to make the point emphatically.[4] Thus even this "liberation" from the empire is cast to fulfill the Torah, even though Pharaoh is not a party to the command of Deuteronomy concerning release.

Second, the imperative is to "ask" for vessels of silver and gold. The notion of a polite request to a taskmaster by slaves seems unlikely. Thus it is more probable (as we shall see) that Yahweh here authorizes the liberated slaves upon leaving to take (steal) something from their overlord class. Surely it was the power elite who owned all the silver and gold accouterments of the good life, whereas the bonded slaves had nothing.

---

3. On the pattern of this command, see David Daube, *The Exodus Pattern in the Bible* (London: Faber and Faber, 1963), especially pp. 55-61.

4. On this text, see Jeffries Mock Hamilton, "Social Justice and Deuteronomy: The Case of Deuteronomy 15" (unpublished dissertation, Princeton Theological Seminary). The infinitive absolutes are as follows: "bless" (v. 4), "hear" (v. 5), "open," "lend" (v. 8), and "give" (v. 10). These forms suggest the intensity and urgency of the practice of release.

The command is a forcible act of equalization authorized by the God who wants the slaves to have not only dignity but wherewithal upon departure.

The speech of Yahweh is followed by a narrative comment about the relative status of "this people" and Pharaoh's Egypt. Two different evaluative statements are made, each of which admits of more than one reading. First, the people received "favor" in the eyes of Egypt. It is far from clear what the statement intends. It could mean that the Egyptians liked this people and were kind to them. Or perhaps it suggests that this people was noticed and feared by the Egyptians, so that the tension between the two is further escalated. While the words themselves suggest a more benign reading, the context scarcely allows for such a reading, because the narrative intends that the tension between the two groups of actors should build further.

In like fashion, the statement about Moses is double-edged: he became "exceedingly great." This characterization is followed by a triad, "in the land," "in the sight of Pharaoh's clique," and "in the sight of the people." "Exceedingly great," however, does not need to suggest that he was widely respected. It can as well mean that Moses was formidable and constituted an enormous threat that the power elite of the empire did not fail to notice. In any case, all these acts and words are preparation for the departure that is to happen soon.

II

The center of the action is in the announcement of the plague (Exod. 11:4-8). Except for the last line of this unit concerning Moses' departure (Exod. 11:8c), this entire unit is a speech of Moses. This speech follows the speech of Yahweh (Exod. 11:1-2) in an odd way. All Yahweh has said is "one more plague," but now Moses describes it in detail. The speech is the speech of Yahweh, "Thus saith the Lord." But we are not told that Moses had received such a speech from Yahweh, only that he spoke it. The speech of Moses attributed to Yahweh is in three parts.

First, Moses describes what will happen to the Egyptians (Exod. 11:4-5). Yahweh's own action is confined to the one powerful participle: "I will go out." Yahweh is about to make an awesome, dreaded move. Yahweh's very presence in itself constitutes a powerful danger. That is all that Yahweh does in this narrative, but it is enough!

From Yahweh's ominous move, there will be two derivative outcomes for the empire. First, there will be death to all the firstborn. The intrusion of death into the narrative in verse 5 is not directly related to Yahweh's action in verse 4, but the connection is clearly intended. Yahweh is a death-bringer. When Yahweh comes, the firstborn of the empire will die. The verse uses the term *firstborn* four times, so that there is a powerful rhetorical emphasis. The first use is generic and inclusive: "all." The second starts at the top of the social scale (Pharaoh), and the last two reach to the bottom of the scale (the firstborn of slaves and livestock). All will die, from A to Z. The devastation is massive. The firstborn are the especially treasured and beloved. The empire will be helpless to protect or keep safe that which it most values and treasures.

Second, the outcome of the wholesale devastation will be a long, loud, terrible cry of wretchedness, grief, lament, rage, and dismay, an unparalleled response to loss. The narrative pictures the whole empire in deep and uncontrolled bereavement. This posture for the empire is so odd because the empire is unaccustomed to loss and grief, always able to prosper and to go from strength to strength. Thus the empire is forced into an awkward mood.

This powerful scene suggests two comments. First, the killing of the firstborn and the great cry wrought in the empire are a close counterpart to the experience of the slaves in Exodus 1–2. In Exodus 1:15-22, Pharaoh decrees the killing of all babies from among the slaves. The devastation now to be worked in the empire is a response in like kind. It is not, however, as massive, because only the firstborn are on the hit list, not all the babies. Second, the cry is a counterpoint to the terrible cry of Israel in its oppression (Exod. 2:23-25). Thus the narrator arranges this announced plague so that it correlates with the earlier abuse of Israel.

Second, the narrative is remarkably restrained in saying what will happen or how it will happen. Indeed, the entire event, though credited to and authorized by God, is shrouded in inscrutable mystery. We are told almost nothing; the narrative surely intends the listener to marvel and trouble at the ominousness of God that is no respecter of persons. Nothing is explained beyond the self-announcement of God's terrible intention.

Third, the narrative does not flinch as we might. It is ruthless and uncompromising. Such a text likely strikes us as a great theological embarrassment. Israel's life, however, begins in this terrible act of compassion and solidarity, which has as its other side an impatient ruthlessness toward this haughty empire. While this may be the narrative of an oppressed community that seeks its own advantage, the voice of that community is taken in the canon as the voice of God, who is utterly allied with this needful people.

In order that we not miss the singular and stunning emphasis of the narrative, verses 4-6 have as their counterpoint verse 7. This verse witnesses to the safety, well-being, and protection that belong to Israel. While death stalks the landscape of the empire in the inscrutable darkness, Israel will not be even minutely disturbed. Indeed, Israel will be so safe, so exempt from the silent intrusion of death, that Israelite dogs will not be awakened. The awesome power of death has eyes in the night and can find its intended object. There will be no mistake, no miscalculation, no accidental death, no killing of innocent "civilians."

In this verse, for the first time in the chapter, the name "Israel" is used to speak of the well-being of this community. Heretofore, the reference had been only to "the people," but as the protection is extended, this guarded, exempt people is finally named. The nameless slaves are called by name as the God of rescue and of death works into the night. Indeed, the contrast is so complete that animals are sorted out like human beings. The animals of Egypt ("livestock") lose their firstborn, and the animals of Israel are safe. The distinction is complete and unerring.

The end of the verse brings us to the central theological affirmation of this entire chapter: ". . . so that you may know. . . ." Who is addressed? We are never told to whom Moses is speaking. In verse 8 the narrative seems to shift and imagine that Moses addresses Egypt. But there are no hints of this earlier. Likely the ostensible address is to Egypt, but the real address is to Israel. Who needs to know about this distinction? While the distinction will be useful information for the empire, it is the benefactors of the dramatic intervention who need to know in order that they may accept their identity and learn to trust the one who acts decisively on their behalf. The Israelites need to know about the distinction made by God so that they do not despair before the imperial presence, so that they do not accept too easily their role as slaves, so that they understand that the destruction of the empire has concrete implications for their socio-political destiny.

The theological claim that God makes a "distinction" is rhetorically enacted by the contrasting ways in which Egypt (Exod. 11:4-6) and Israel (Exod. 11:7a) are treated. Thus the distinction is already enacted before we arrive at this announcement. Egypt is assaulted by the God who goes out at midnight, whereas Israel is left undisturbed. That is the primal distinction in this narrative. Nothing more is said or made of "the distinction," that is, nothing is said of "election" or an enduring status or a special relation to God. In the context of the entire Exodus-Sinai narrative, of course, much more is claimed than is here likely implied. In Exodus 19:5-6, the enduring, special status of Israel is anticipated, but that special status is completely dependent upon covenant obedience, which in our passage is not even mentioned. The distinction made here in the dark of the night has no connection to obedience.

Because this entire chapter pivots on this claim of distinction, we may usefully pause over the assertion. There are twin problematics in making this assertion a source for a larger theological claim. On the one hand, the notion of "special people" in some circles is objectionable because it smacks of partisanship and opposes a religion of evenhanded tolerance. Such an objection, of course, applies not only to this text but to the Bible as a whole. Indeed, the Bible focuses precisely on such a "scandal of particularity." The claim without which the Bible cannot do is that God does choose in a partisan way. (A comparable, perhaps more intense claim is made in the New Testament concerning Jesus of Nazareth, who is confessed as God's special choice as Messiah.)[5] In both the Hebrew Bible and in the New Testament, such special choosing is indispensable and requires that our notion of evenhanded tolerance be revised. To be sure, such a claim for a "distinct people" does not remove from God's horizon other peoples, as is evident even in Exodus 19:6. The Bible continues to struggle with the twofold claim that God both governs and cares for all peoples and that God makes a distinction in preference for this community.

This leads us, on the other hand, to the second problem in the claim of distinction. Such a claim can be construed in a narrow, triumphalist way as though this community holds a monopoly on God's attentiveness. That is, the special status of this community on occasion leads to a notion that no other people receives good from God.

In the text itself we are given no clue about the character of this people or the nature of the distinction. There are two ways to construe this distinction that live in some tension with each other. On the one hand, the obvious reading of the distinction is to understand Israel's undisturbed sleep in this narrative as *ethnic*. That is, the distinguished people is the Jewish community, which is reckoned as a special nation. There is no doubt that

---

5. On the claims made for Jesus in the categories of contemporary Judaism, see Paul M. van Buren, *A Theology of the Jewish-Christian Reality 3* (San Francisco: Harper and Row, 1988).

later texts in the tradition move in this direction. Caution about that reading here may be indicated by the fact that before verse 7, the slaves addressed by this narrative are never called "Israel" but in verses 2, 3 are "the people." The narrative is not quick to identify this community. They are "Israelites" only in the verse where the distinction is made, suggesting that it is the act of Yahweh, and not any social or national marking, that forms Israel. Moreover, the historical evidence concerning the origin of Israel suggests that Israel is formed by the covenanting of God with all sorts of desperate peoples, without reference to race or nation.[6] Thus the formation of Israel from a "mixed crowd" (Exod. 12:38) suggests that this community is formed as a theological act without reference to ethnic identity.

On the other hand, a case can be made that Israel is essentially a sociological phenomenon in this early tradition. That is, "Israel" comprises all the socio-economically marginalized peoples who are gathered together around the presence and promise of Yahweh against the established power of Egypt. This reading can claim support in this text because the contrast in verse 2 seems to be between those who have silver and gold and those who may now take it. The sociological analysis of early Israel suggests something like a "class reading" in which the have-nots emerge from the midst of the haves.[7]

Thus it seems plausible that the people formed by the distinction of God are people who in socio-economic categories are "losers," cut off from conventional forms of power that the Egyptian royal establishment had used vigorously against them. There is no doubt that the tradition evolves toward an ethnic or national identity, but it does not begin clearly at that point.

Such a delicate and nuanced reading of *distinction* opens two important possibilities. First, it asserts that Israel as God's beloved people is a

6. Norman K. Gottwald, *The Tribes of Yahweh* (Maryknoll, N.Y.: Orbis Books, 1979): 467-76 and passim, has most clearly argued that early Israel is not an ethnic community but that the "tribes" of Israel are coalitions of those with a shared social agenda. The "covenant" is a mode of social relations that cuts across all ethnic groupings.

7. Gottwald, *The Tribes of Yahweh*, 467, juxtaposes "urban statism" and "rural tribalism" as categories for such a class analysis. See also Marvin L. Chaney, "Ancient Palestinian Peasant Movements and the Formation of Premonarchic Israel," *Palestine in Transition: The Emergence of Ancient Israel*, ed. David Noel Freedman and David Frank Graf, The Social World of Biblical Antiquity Series 2 (Sheffield: Almond Press, 1983): 39-90.

theological mystery wrought out of God's inexplicable decision.[8] Israel is not and never was a nation or a nation-state like any other nation (cf. 1 Sam. 8:5, 20). Those who would understand Israel must ponder how in this situation of exploitation God in peculiar and powerful ways attended to the outsiders of the empire.

Second, as this distinctive people is understood theologically and not first of all ethnically, it opens the way to the *mystery of Israel* being a model and paradigm and not a closed off case without possible replication.[9] That is, as God has sided with this needful band to give an unexpected future, so the way is open for God to work such a distinction again and again in other contexts, for other groups of people who stand helpless in the face of brutal power (cf. Amos 9:7).[10] Without denying that this theological mystery emerges in and around and for the sake of Israel, such a view suggests that the same God can indeed continue to make such distinctions in other contexts for the sake of other communities.

III

The contrasting actions of God in verses 4-6 and verse 7*a* make the different destinies of Egypt and Israel abundantly clear, even to the Egyptians (Exod. 11:8). Verse 8 constitutes something of a rhetorical, dramatic problem, even though its intent is quite clear. Ostensibly this is a continuation of Moses' speech begun in verse 4. However, in verse 4 we are not told to whom Moses speaks, and in verses 5-6 Moses never addresses the Egyptians directly in the second person. Thus there is a slip in rhetoric, for in verse 8, Moses now seems to be addressing Pharaoh and his company directly. The narrative makes the anticipated response of Pharaoh to be words in the mouth of Moses.

This peculiar verse (which without acknowledgement places Moses

8. Martin Buber in many places has written of the theological mystery of Israel. See, for example, "Holy Event," in *On the Bible: Eighteen Studies* (New York: Schocken Books, 1968): 63-79, and "The Election of Israel: A Biblical Inquiry," ibid., 80-92.

9. Paul M. van Buren, *A Theology of the Jewish-Christian Reality Part 2* (San Francisco: Harper and Row, 1983): 179-83, suggests that the mystery of Israel can, indeed, serve as a model and suggestion for a like history and faith among blacks. I take van Buren's point about Jews and blacks as capable of extrapolation from Jews to other communities as well.

10. Amos intends to combat Israel's pride in its distinctiveness; cf. Matt. 3:10.

in the presence of Pharaoh) serves in two ways to complete the earlier anticipation of the chapter. In verse 1 God has promised that Pharaoh would let Israel go or even drive God's people out; now it is affirmed that Pharaoh will do so. In verse 3 Moses is a man of "great importance"; now Egypt bows low to him. Perhaps the most noteworthy rhetorical feature in this verse is the threefold use of the Exodus term ("to leave") in this verse:

> Leave!
> I will leave.
> He left Pharaoh.

This is indeed a verse about leaving, that is, the Exodus verb "to go out" is utilized as though the narrative is preparing the listener for what is to follow in the larger narrative.

In any case, Pharaoh now urges Israel to depart, according to the anticipation of Moses. Moses in "hot anger" departs Pharaoh. We are not told why Moses is angry. The issue has been joined between the two, the distinction made by God has been enacted. The narrative traces the subtle way whereby power is slowly but surely shifting from Pharaoh (who is increasingly helpless) to Moses (who is increasingly authorized and emboldened).

IV

With the anticipation of verse 1 and the speech of Moses in verse 8, we are not prepared for verses 9-10. It is as though these verses promptly negate the gains claimed in verses 1-8. The same Pharaoh who had, according to Moses, used the Exodus word in verse 8 now will not listen. His not listening, however, is not only Pharaoh's stubbornness. Indeed, not listening is posited as part of Yahweh's plan. "Not listening" in order that Yahweh may do more acts of wondrous power that demonstrate sovereignty. If the Exodus had been permitted at this point in the narrative, there would be no need or occasion for Yahweh's show of power, no reason for the strike of death at night that here is announced.

Thus the narrator engages in a delaying tactic. The power of Yahweh is now clear and beyond challenge. Yahweh, however, works both sides of the street. Yahweh not only challenges Pharaoh with a show of power, but Yahweh also enhances the resistance of Pharaoh. Yahweh is the one who causes Pharaoh to have a resistant heart and to refuse the departure of Israel. By the time we reach the end of this chapter, the lines are clearly drawn. We have no reason to doubt the resolve and capacity of Yahweh, but the crisis has not yet ripened to fruition. Everything is in readiness, and we are left to wait.

The wait is not long. The tradition includes ritual provisions (Exod. 12:1-28). The narrative itself resumes in Exodus 12:29-32. There the last plague happens, as chapter 11 has anticipated. Yahweh strikes all the firstborn of Egypt, as Moses had said. There is a cry of death, as Moses had said. The empire is effectively immobilized (Exod. 12:29-30). When the moment of departure is finally reached, the scene is short and terse. Pharaoh authorizes and urges the Israelites to go away (Exod. 12:31), just as Moses had said. Now the Israelites do go, but not before they confiscate silver and gold of Egypt, as God had authorized (Exod. 12:35-36). Finally the verb "to plunder" is used. It is not a polite request but a violent, hurried seizure of silver and gold. Israel is on its way . . . to freedom!

V

Preaching this text may pose some preliminary problems: *(a)* Some will resist the affirmation that freedom is wrought through violence, including the confiscation of property; *(b)* verse 8 offers some dramatic confusion that is impossible to smooth out; *(c)* Yahweh hardens Pharaoh's heart to make the dispute even more difficult, so that Yahweh seems to act against Yahweh's own resolve of emancipation.[11] These matters are minor in the context of the larger narrative. The narrative bears unmistakable and un- avoidable witness to one claim: The God of Israel is powerfully, actively, decisively, violently present in a situation of exploitation, on the side of freedom for the exploited. Thus in narrative fashion, God is sketched out in all God's dangerous, passionate freedom.

In pondering the common preaching of Jews and Christians, I antici- pate that different problems face the two preaching communities. On the one hand, Jews will have no problem in taking this narrative as their own, though perhaps some would rather pass over lightly the crucial role of

---

11. On "hardness of heart," see Brevard S. Childs, *The Book of Exodus,* 170-75, and Gerhard von Rad, *Old Testament Theology II* (San Francisco: Harper and Row, 1965): 151-55.

violence in the narrative. The preaching issue, I suggest, is that this story is not the monopoly of Jews but is a witness of the God of Israel and to the characteristic way in which God keeps working in hard ways for the freedom of the oppressed. Thus the narrative can be held so closely and intensely that one resists the ongoing power of the narrative to assert that (a) this is what God characteristically does and (b) the human process is an ongoing story of God's intentions against oppression for the sake of freedom where we do not notice or confess it and where we may not even welcome it. There are still dark nights when the power of death works its way against the oppressor.[12]

The preaching issues with Christians, I suggest, are very different. Christians will not make the mistake of claiming this narrative as excessively their own. The Christian temptation rather is to resist the violence inherent in the story, and particularly the violence that is the work of Yahweh. Partly that response is because of a revulsion to violence and a refusal to see that the Egyptian empire in its entire socio-economic arrangement is a violence machine and the intrusion of Yahweh is a responding violence necessary to emancipation.[13] Partly the response is an affront that God should be so intimately drawn into the concreteness of human affairs in such a partisan way. The perpetrators of the abuse now become its victims. As the first become last, so the perpetrator becomes the victim. This inversion is echoed in the teaching of Jesus, which now can be heard in its tone of ominous threat:

> Blessed are those who weep now, for you will laugh. . . .
> Woe to you who are laughing now, for you will mourn and weep.
>
> (Luke 6:21, 26)

Israel is the community that weeps now but will laugh later. Egypt is the community that laughs now and will weep later. The futures and destinies of both peoples are radically and drastically revised. This is to harden the claim excessively. This text does not generalize but only asserts that,

---

12. On the continuing pertinence of this tradition, see Michael Walzer, *Exodus and Revolution* (New York: Basic Books, 1985), and Bas van Iersel and Anton Weiier, *Exodus: A Lasting Paradigm* (Edinburgh: T. & T. Clark, 1987).

13. On the state's decisive role in social violence, see Robert McAfee Brown, *Religion and Violence,* 2nd ed. (Philadelphia: Westminster Press, 1987), and Helder Camara, *Spiral of Violence* (Denvelle, N.J.: Dimension Books, 1971). Brown offers a helpful bibliography.

vis-à-vis the oppressive empire, God notices and acts. Biblical faith must endlessly negotiate its way between a broad tolerance that dismisses the distinction and a triumphalism that overstates the distinction. Thus the response is in part an ideological naiveté about social processes and in part a defense of a God that has long been too safe.

Preaching this text requires the listening community (including both Jews and Christians) to hear the whole plot and to credit all its characters in a drama of liberation. Christians may be helped to enter the narrative by noticing the parallel narratives in which Jesus enacts destructive violence against demonic forces that deny full humanness to the subjects of the stories.[14]

This story invites a rethink of faith for both Jews and Christians. In the end, this narrative is not about a distinct people nor about an offensive act of violence. It is a witness to the character and purpose of God who is presented as an effective agent in the life of both empire and slaves, who makes a decisive difference in the life of both, and who by intervention (against Egypt) and exemption (on behalf of the slaves) decisively reconfigures the life of both. Assent to this story has spinoffs in terms of distinctiveness and liberation. At its center, however, is the insistence that the life of the world in its oppression and in its emancipation, in its distribution of goods and of dignity, must be radically retold because of this God whose intention is strong enough to thwart the empire and alternative enough to send the slaves free from bondage, not empty-handed.

The story must not be explained. It happens in the night, hidden from our scrutiny and our understanding. God's ways are sometimes manifest; in this story, however, neither empire nor slave community can know how the turn happens. The empire can only cry at its resulting loss. The slave community can only sing at its new life. Neither the crying empire nor the singing slaves can see the God who intrudes. They can only tell the story, with all its terrible losses and wondrous gains, losses and gains not permitted by the empire, not imagined by the slaves.

14. See Ched Myers, *Binding the Strong Man: A Political Reading of Mark's Story of Jesus* (Maryknoll, N.Y.: Orbis Books, 1990), and Walter Wink, *Naming the Powers: The Language of Power in the New Testament, I* (Philadelphia: Fortress Press, 1984).

Changing God's Mind

DONALD E. GOWAN

"God really does respond to us. . . .
God is willing to change."

This text claims that certain widely held understandings of God are in fact caricatures. Behind the questions, "Why me, Lord?" or "How could God do this to me?" frequently lies either a picture of an oriental potentate, a great king sitting on his throne handing down decrees without concern for how they affect the lives of his subjects, or the picture of a judge pronouncing sentences, unmoved personally by what will become of those pronounced guilty. It is true that in Exodus 32:7-14 God begins by pronouncing Israel guilty and that Scripture does speak of God as king and as judge. The pictures many people carry with them of the arbitrary king or the impartial judge are immediately challenged by this passage, however, when God first consults with a human being before deciding — indeed seems to ask Moses' permission! — and when at the end the human being succeeds in changing God's mind.

Such a story can be misread so as to produce other caricatures, and so we shall need to proceed carefully. Passages such as this have been taken as evidence for a God who is less concerned about mercy than humans are, and they may also be read as corresponding to a concept of a trickster, completely amoral, or a blunderer, reacting to set straight his first inept efforts. The value of this text is that, when taken with the utmost seriousness, without trying to explain away what it explicitly says about God within the context of the debacle of the golden calf incident, it challenges us to believe in a God who is fully in charge yet open to human intervention, a God who is the maintainer of justice but who must be known by words that have no relationship to justice: compassionate and merciful (Exod. 34:6).

The story of the golden calf has attracted great interest and has a long history of interpretation, including a great body of contemporary, scholarly discussion, but the whole story does not need to be discussed in detail here.[1] A few words must be said about the enormity of the sin, as described in Exodus and as understood by all later interpreters, however, for this provides the essential context for the dialogue between Moses and God. The covenant had just been ratified, less than forty days earlier. It involved the promise of an exclusive relationship: "Now therefore, if you obey my voice and keep my covenant, you shall be my treasured possession out of all the peoples. Indeed, the whole earth is mine, but you shall be for me a priestly kingdom and a holy nation" (Exod. 19:5-6). And the people all answered as one: "Everything that the Lord has spoken we will do" (Exod. 19:8). The golden calf is seen by Moses and by the author of the passage as a direct violation of the first two commandments, and those commandments have always been understood by Jews to contain the essence of God's requirements of them: No other God but Yahweh and no physical representations of anything claimed to be god.[2]

But forty days later the relationship has already been broken, and when one breaks a relationship that was supposed to be exclusive, as this was, the effects will be severe. As Amos put it, "You only have I known of all the families of the earth; therefore I will punish you for all your iniquities" (Amos 3:2). Terence Fretheim appropriately compares the relationship to marriage, as the Old Testament already does, and the golden calf incident to the pain of divorce.[3] The rabbis, given their commitment to one God who could not be represented by anything in heaven or on earth, considered the golden calf to be the worst sin ever committed by Israel. *Exodus Rabbah* says, "Had Israel waited for Moses and not perpetrated that act, there would have been no exile, neither would the Angel

1. L. Smolar & M. Aberbach, "The Golden Calf Episode in Postbiblical Literature," *HUCA,* 39 (1968): 91-116.

2. Compare Deuteronomy's interpretation of the two commandments in 6:4 and 4:15-16; and *Ex. Rab.* XLII.8.

3. Terence E. Fretheim, *Exodus,* Interpretation (Louisville, Ky.: John Knox, 1991): 284.

of Death have had any power over them" (XXXII:1; cf. XLIII.2). It is thus as close as Judaism gets to a concept of original sin; and so Fretheim speaks of this as Judaism's "fall story."[4]

Potentially, then, the first six verses of chapter 32 might have led to the appearance of one of Scripture's repeated themes: starting over. That is, in fact, what God proposes to do in verse 10: "Now therefore let me alone, that my wrath may burn hot against them and I may consume them; and of you I will make a great nation." Starting over is an important biblical theme but not the dominant one. I was first led to consider where it appears in Scripture when I was writing my commentary on Genesis 1–11 and had to deal with the significance of the Flood story, the first example of starting over.[5]

At the end, the author has to admit the Flood really served no purpose and was thus not to be understood as revealing God's way of bringing about the cure for human sin. God had wiped out the wicked and was about to start over with one righteous man and his family, but then he must admit, "I will never again curse the ground because of humankind, for the inclination of the human heart is evil from youth; nor will I ever again destroy every living creature as I have done" (Gen. 8:21). And the drunkenness of Noah, in the next chapter, is the first example of the truth that the inclination is evil from youth and that sin will have to be dealt with in some other way. The history of salvation begins not with the rainbow covenant in Genesis 9 but with the promise to Abraham, and it proves to be a long and difficult process. The theme of starting over does reappear, however, most prominently in the message of the prophets, who interpreted the exile as the death of old Israel and then promised that God would start over with resurrection in the form of a new, forgiven people. And the later apocalyptic writers also thought of God one day carrying out a dramatic wiping out of all evil to replace it with a new creation.

But that theme stands in tension throughout Scripture with the other one, represented by the working out of the promise to Abraham, and this latter one tends to dominate, as the wording of God's reflection on the Flood already predicts (Gen. 8:21-22 and 9:8-17). The slow and difficult process we call the history of salvation is the basic Old Testament story and is the central message of the New Testament's teaching of salvation

4. Fretheim, *Exodus*, 279.
5. Donald E. Gowan, *Genesis 1–11: From Eden to Babel*, International Theological Commentary (Grand Rapids: Eerdmans, 1988): 100-101.

through grace. "While we were still weak," Paul says, "Christ died for the ungodly" (Rom. 5:6) — instead of wrath burning hot against us. The history of salvation emphasizes God's attributes of patience, mercy, and forgiveness, and the tension between the two biblical themes — starting over by wiping out the sinful and bearing with the sinful in the effort to redeem them — is typically expressed in theology as the tension between justice and mercy. Nowhere in the Bible is that tension expressed more compactly and thus more forcefully than in Exodus 32–34.

We are concentrating on Exodus 32:7-14 because of the occurrence of two words: *hannihah,* "let (me) alone," in verse 10, and *hinnahem,* "repent" (better, with NRSV, "change your mind") in verse 12. This is one of the most striking passages in the whole Bible concerning what may be called the "vulnerability" of God. Having said that, I must immediately emphasize that in this passage God's vulnerability is set alongside strong statements concerning his sovereignty. God appears in verses 7-10 as the judge who pronounces Israel guilty, worthy of annihilation. A few verses later the freedom of God is declared in the classic statement, "I will be gracious to whom I will be gracious, and will show mercy on whom I will show mercy" (Exod. 33:19). And the covenant eventually is renewed without any request by Moses or the people, by the initiative of God alone (Exod. 34:10). Yet, this sovereign God, who is fully in charge according to most of the verses in this section (Exod. 32–34), not only listens to the appeals of Moses and grants them — albeit in accordance with God's own freedom to modify them (cf. Exod. 33:18-23) — but is also represented as a God who will change plans as a result of human intervention, and more than that; he indicates that he has subjected himself to some extent to the will of Moses. There has been a good deal of discussion over the centuries of the attribution of "repentance" to God, and I will come to that shortly, but not so much has been done with the "let me alone" of verse 10, very likely because it doesn't fit most people's theology very well. I intend to take them both seriously.

Moses has been on the mountain forty days and the people have given up on him. "As for this Moses, the man who brought us up out of the land of Egypt, we do not know what has become of him" (Exod. 32:1b). But they have really given up on Yahweh, as God sees it. Having made them his people forty days earlier, Yahweh now will not call them "my people." They are "your people" in verse 7 and "this people" in verse 9. They have turned aside quickly from the way God commanded them, and they have corrupted themselves (NRSV, "acted perversely"). The root is the same one

used in the prelude to the Flood story: "And God saw that the earth was
corrupt; for all flesh had corrupted its ways upon the earth" (Gen. 6:12).
In Genesis 6:13 the narrator uses the same root to describe what God will
do: "now I am going to destroy them along with the earth." The root seems
to describe something like a physical corruption, such as rot, which destroys
the thing corrupted. But the people at Sinai have insisted on it: "I have
seen this people, and behold, it is a stiff-necked people" (Exod. 32:9).
There is judgment even in the choice of the common word *see* at this point.
Exodus speaks rarely about what God has seen. In Exodus 2:25; 3:7; and
4:31, God saw the misery of Israel in Egypt, and that led to God's deter-
mination to save them. God saw Moses approach the burning bush (Exod.
3:4), and God saw the blood on the doorposts on the Passover night (Exod.
12:13). Divine seeing is a part of the gracious, saving acts of God, until
chapter 32, but now God sees "it is a stiff-necked people" he has chosen.
Seeing already involves a decision. The decision corresponds to justice. In
their preference for the golden calf, they have rejected the way of life, so
they should die. That need not mean God has failed, for God is free to
choose a person or a people, and God means to choose Moses, just as long
before God had chosen to start over with one righteous man, Noah, and
just as God had freely chosen Abraham and Sarah to be the recipients of
the gracious promise. Indeed, the offer to Moses is a clear reflection of the
promise to Abraham: "of you I will make a great nation" (cf. Gen. 12:2).

There is something new in this passage, however. Noah and Abraham
had no choice in the matter, but Moses does. God has to get Moses'
permission, believe it or not. Moses hasn't said anything yet, is still on the
mountain, and knew nothing of what was going on down below until God
told him about it; but God strangely does not feel free to act without
consulting Moses: "Now therefore let me alone, that my wrath may burn
hot against them and I may consume them; and of you I will make a great
nation." What shall we make of this?

First, let us see what the word means. It is a hifil imperative of a
Hebrew root, which means to let something lie in a place, to leave behind,
to let something remain, to allow something to happen, or, in five occurrences, all in the imperative, to let someone alone. The blind Samson says
to the guard who is holding him, "Let me alone that I may feel the pillars
supporting the house" (Judg. 16:26). David says to those who would kill
Shimei for cursing him, "Let him alone and let him curse" (2 Sam. 16:11).
Josiah uses the expression with reference to the remains of a prophet whose
tomb is found at Bethel, "Let him alone, let no one move his bones"

(2 Kings 23:18). And God says through Hosea, "Like a stubborn heifer, Israel is stubborn; can the Lord now feed them like a lamb in a broad pasture? Ephraim is joined to idols — let him alone" (Hos. 4:16-17). These are the other occurrences. In each case someone who has the power to do something to another is asked to refrain. Only once in the Bible is God the one affected, as he asks of a human being, "Let me alone. . . ."[6] I find it astonishing that anyone dared to write such a thing.

As you might expect, interpreters have either glossed over the expression, saying nothing about it, or have said this is an example of God accommodating our human inability to understand him in his fullness. Calvin, who used this principle of accommodation to good effect in many places and who does so with reference to God's repentance (Exod. 32:12), does not seem to be as alarmed at this expression as we might anticipate.

> Hence we gather that His secret judgments are a great deep; whilst, at the same time, His will is declared to us in His word as far as suffices for our edification in faith and piety. And this is more clearly expressed by the context; for He asks of Moses to let Him alone. Now, what does this mean? Is it not that, unless He should obtain a truce from a human being, He will not be able freely to execute His vengeance? — adopting, that is to say, by this mode of expression the character of another, He declares His high estimation of His servant, to whose prayers He pays such deference as to say that they are a hinderance to Him. Thus it is said in Psalm cvi.23, that Moses "stood in the breach, to turn away the wrath" of God. Hence do we plainly perceive the wonderful goodness of God, who not only hears the prayers of His people when they humbly call upon Him, but suffers them to be in a manner intercessors with Him.[7]

Calvin is speaking of accommodation here, without using the word, so he would not go as far as some modern interpreters in deducing something about the character of God from these verses, but he is certainly on the right track in recognizing that here is to be found an important teaching on prayer. I shall be drawing two conclusions from this passage. The one,

6. Deuteronomy does not soften it, as the story is retold in 9:8-21. A synonym, the hifil of *rph*, is used, and that term is also used of God only in this text.

7. John Calvin, *Commentaries on the Four Last Books of Moses Arranged in the Form of a Harmony* (Grand Rapids: Eerdmans, 1950): III.341.

on the possibility of petitionary and intercessory prayer, is in agreement
with Calvin and other traditional interpreters; the other, on divine changeability or vulnerability, is only in our time being taken up with some
boldness by certain interpreters. For the time being, let us stay with the
plain meaning of the words in verse 10 and allow that God is, for some
reason, unwilling to act without Moses' permission.[8]

Calvin will not gloss over the scandal of the passage. He sees God's
intention to be done with Israel and to start over with Moses as a test of
Moses' faith, and he associates that with his own knowledge of events that
threaten to shake the faith of Christian leaders.

> This was, indeed, the sharpest and sorest trial of the faith of Moses; when
> God seemed to contradict Himself and to depart from His covenant. If
> ever, after having been long oppressed by excessive calamities, we are
> not only wearied by the delay, but also agitated with various doubts,
> which at length tempt us to despair, as if God had disappointed us by
> deceptive promises, the contest is severe and terrible; but when God
> seems at first sight to throw discredit upon His own words, we have
> need of unusual fortitude and firmness to sustain this assault.[9]

And he continues in this vein for another page.

Moses disobeys. He will not let God alone. In one of George Coats'
articles on Exodus he discusses this passage as one of the striking examples
of how faithfulness sometimes must be expressed by challenging God,
rather than meekly obeying. But how does one know what distinguishes
an accusation addressed to God as an act of loyal trust and faith from one
that can be taken only as rebellion or apostasy? This and other passages,
such as the first chapter of Habakkuk, support his conclusion that to contend
with God is the mark of an obedient servant when it is based on the
conviction that God will live up to his reputation and the conviction that
God will keep his promises.[10] We shall see that Moses does begin with

8. The more common, and less startling, interpretation is to take this as God's
invitation to Moses to intercede: "Exodus," *The Pentateuch and Rashi's Commentary:
A Linear Translation into English,* by Rabbi Abraham ben Isaiah and Rabbi Benjamin
Sharfman (Brooklyn: S. S. & R. Publishing Co., 1949): 405; Herbert Chanan Brichto,
"The Worship of the Golden Calf: A Literary Analysis of a Fable on Idolatry" *HUCA,*
44 (1983): 9.

9. Calvin, *Commentaries,* III.339f.

10. George W. Coats, "The King's Loyal Opposition: Obedience and Authority

reputation but that his clinching argument has to do with God's faithfulness
to his promise.

Moses has three points. They have been neatly labeled by Fretheim
as (1) reasonableness, (2) reputation, and (3) promise.[11] The first two begin
with a familiar word from the laments, "Why?" and we recognize from
this and other features that Moses does in fact use elements of Israel's
traditional language of prayer.

> O Lord, why does thy wrath burn hot against thy people, whom thou
> hast brought forth out of the land of Egypt with great power and with a
> mighty hand? (Exod. 32:11)

God has gone to considerable trouble to get them this far. They didn't really
want to come, in the first place, and once they hit the wilderness they
wanted to go back. Pharaoh took even more persuading than the Israelites,
and the plagues and crossing of the sea showed that even the cosmos itself
had to be disrupted in order to bring this about. Certainly the golden calf
is far worse than the earlier incidents of "murmuring in the wilderness"
(Exod. 15:22–16:12), but shouldn't God reconsider this new plan? Isn't
God overreacting? Be reasonable, Moses dares to say to God.

Next he asks God to consider what the neighbors will say:

> Why should the Egyptians say, "With evil intent did he bring them forth,
> to slay them in the mountains, and to consume them from the face of
> the earth"? (Exod. 32:12*a*)

It makes a difference, in Israel, what the nations think of their God. Deuteronomy's version of Moses' plea introduces yet another insult that might
come from Egypt, no doubt based on what foreigners who had defeated
Israel actually did say, in later times: ". . . otherwise the land from which
you have brought us might say, 'Because the Lord was not able to bring
them into the land that he promised them' . . ." (Deut. 9:28). During the
exile Ezekiel expressed great concern for the kind of witness Israel had
made to the nations. So far it has all been negative, he concluded, but when
the restoration comes, "then the nations will know that I am Yahweh" (cf.

---

in Exodus 32–34" in *Canon and Authority,* ed. George W. Coats & Burke O. Long
(Philadelphia: Fortress Press, 1977): 91-109.

  11. Fretheim, *Exodus,* 285.

Ezek. 34:30; 36:36). In the meantime Ezekiel accounts for Yahweh's
patience in bearing with rebellious Israel in the wilderness in accordance
with Moses' argument: "But I acted for the sake of my name, that it should
not be profaned in the sight of the nations among whom they lived, in
whose sight I made myself known to them in bringing them out of the land
of Egypt" (Ezek. 20:9).

Then come four potent verbs, as Moses moves to his third argument
(Exod. 32:12*b*-13): turn (*shuv*), the common verb used of human repentance; repent (the niphal of *nhm*), better translated with the NRSV "change
your mind"; remember (*zkr*); and swear (the niphal of *shv'*). Let us take
them in reverse order, understanding *turn* and *repent* to be synonymous
here. Biblical Hebrew has no word that literally means "promise," but the
Old Testament is full of promises, nevertheless. The most potent word in
the language associated with the idea of promising is "to swear, to take a
solemn oath." Moses' quotation of the divine promise is not an exact
citation of anything in Genesis, but most of what he says may be found by
combining Genesis 22:16-17 with Genesis 12:7 or 15:18. A major repeating
theme from Genesis 12 through the wilderness materials in Numbers is the
jeopardizing of that promise, with one incident after another raising the
question whether God would, or could, fulfill it. It might be fair to say that
the command to sacrifice Isaac in Genesis 22 and this story of the golden
calf represent the most critical threats to the promise in the Torah, and it
is significant that the first represents those times in Israel's experience when
it seemed that God had put the promise in jeopardy, while the second
represents the more frequent occasions when the threat to the promise is
Israel's own doing. The disturbing truth, to us and to Israel, about the
freedom of God underlies this theme. God himself has taken a solemn oath
— how could that ever be broken? Doesn't that mean God is committed
to us, no matter what may happen, including anything we may do? That
we, and Israel, would like to believe, but that kind of security is regularly
undercut by passages such as this one. The God who is truly God is free
to change his mind and without such freedom would be something less
than God. That is not particularly good news to us, it keeps us on edge,
but that is without question the God we find in these chapters.

Moses, however, appeals to God's solemn oath, as the clinching argument that God should not give up on Israel. Yes, God has the right and the
power to start over, but that is not the way God has been working with the
descendants of Abraham. In a way, this is a very weak argument, for God has
offered to start over with Moses, who is a descendent of Abraham, Isaac, and

Jacob, and who could keep the line intact. So maybe the key word in verse 13 is *remember. Remember* is used in a special way with God as subject. It is not as if it were thought that God's memory was faulty when he is called upon to remember or when God is said to have remembered. One of the uses of *zkr* in Hebrew has to do with the decision to take action, and, typically, it is used of God in that way. God is the subject of the verb only three times in Exodus. It is associated with three other potent verbs in 2:24-25:

> And God *heard* their groaning, and God *remembered* his covenant with Abraham, with Isaac, and with Jacob. And God *saw* the people of Israel, and God *knew* their condition.

We have already observed the contrast in the use of "see" between chapters 2 and 32. *Know* is also a common word but is used with God as subject in only a few significant places in Exodus (in the immediate context, 33:12, 17). And *remember* occurs only with reference to the covenant with the patriarchs. The other passage is Exodus 6:5:

> Moreover I have heard the groaning of the people of Israel whom the Egyptians hold in bondage and I have remembered my covenant.

The occurrences in chapters 2 and 6 mark God's decision to begin the exodus, the first step toward fulfilling the promise to Abraham, Isaac, and Jacob, which the oppression in Egypt seemed to have made a thing of the past. It had begun; Moses appeals to God to let it continue somehow. He cannot defend Israel: they are guilty and do not deserve to go on. If the justice of God were the subject there could be no argument; the matter is clear. Moses can appeal to no ground for continuance in Israel, but he believes there is a ground in the character of Yahweh. That allows him to ask God to change his mind.

Fretheim and Jeremias have written special studies of the so-called repentance of God,[12] and there is a thorough excursus on the subject in the commentary on Amos by Andersen and Freedman.[13] Brueggemann and I

---

12. Terence E. Fretheim, "The Repentance of God: A Key to Evaluating Old Testament God-talk," *Horizons in Biblical Theology,* 10 (1988): 47-70, and Jörg Jeremias, *Die Reue Gottes: Aspecte der alttestamentliche Gottesvorstellung* (Neukirchener Verlag, 1975).

13. Francis I. Andersen and David N. Freedman, *Amos,* AB (New York: Doubleday, 1989): 638-79.

have also discussed it briefly in our Genesis commentaries, in connection with its first occurrence, Genesis 6:6, the prelude to the Flood story.[14] The KJV translated that verse, "and it repented the Lord that he had made man on the earth, and it grieved him at his heart," trying to find a passive sense for the niphal stem of the root *nhm.* Now we recognize that the niphal of that root is active, so the RSV, the NRSV, and other modern versions translate, "and the Lord was sorry." Elsewhere, however, the RSV frequently used "repent" in the active voice but occasionally chose "relent" or "change his mind." The NRSV has now appropriately abandoned "repent" when God is the subject, as he usually is, for the English word carries undesirable connotations. We ordinarily use it to speak of repenting of sin, and it is never said in the Bible that God sins or needs to repent of sin. There are two other English words beginning with *re-* that convey the appropriate connotations: *regret* and *relent.*

The statistics on the use of this term are important. It occurs thirty-six times. Thirty times God is the subject; humans are the subject six times. Twice the human subject repents of sin (Jer. 8:6; 31:19); the other references speak of change of mind or regret, like those in which God is subject.[15]

This is one of the more unusual ways of speaking of God's mercy. Of the thirty occurrences with God as subject, twenty-four of them speak of God changing his mind, and in nineteen of those God changes his mind away from an intended or actual judgment of sinful people. Among the other five uses, only one is from mercy to judgment. Jeremiah proposes a hypothetical case, claiming that if a nation does evil, God will change his mind about his intended blessings. In two passages the word is used twice each to speak of God's regret that something intended for good has not worked out: the creation of human beings (Gen. 6:6, 7) and the selection of Saul to be king (1 Sam. 15:11, 35).

The other six occurrences speak of God not changing his mind. Jeremiah and Ezekiel claim that the imminent judgment they proclaim cannot be averted (Jer. 4:28; 20:16; Ezek. 24:14), and Zechariah refers back to that judgment (Zech. 8:14). In Psalm 110:4 God affirms that he will never change his mind about the oath to the house of David: "You are a priest forever according to the order of Melchizedek." This leaves the most

14. Walter Brueggemann, *Genesis,* Interpretation (Richmond: John Knox, 1982): 77-81; Donald Gowan, *Genesis 1–11,* 92-95.

15. The normal word for human repentance is *shuv,* and that does appear in Exod. 32:12, in an unusual usage, with God as subject, as a synonym for *hinnahem.*

puzzling of such statements, for it is very general and it occurs in 1 Samuel 15, right in the midst of the story in which it is said twice that God did change his mind about Saul. Samuel is relentless, in spite of Saul's confession of sin and appeal for forgiveness; God has rejected him. And the finality of that is sealed by this theological statement: "Moreover the Glory of Israel will not recant or change his mind; for he is not a mortal, that he should change his mind" (1 Sam. 15:29).

Does the chapter contradict itself? Fretheim claims it does not.[16] He sees this as a classic example of our inability ever to express the full truth about God in human language. Whereas Calvin approached the matter from the divine direction, speaking of God's accommodation of his speech to our meager capacities of understanding, the modern way is to approach it from the human direction, via linguistic studies of the uses of metaphor. The ideas of regretting or changing one's mind come from human experience; they can be no more than imperfect metaphors for what God is really like, but they do convey a measure of truth. So Fretheim says the two apparently contrary uses of *hinnahem* are evidence of the discontinuity between human metaphors and divine reality. In 1 Samuel 15:29 and again in Numbers 23:19 it is said that God does not change his mind, because he is not a human being. But in Hosea 11, when God *does* change his mind, saying "I will not execute my fierce anger; I will not again destroy Ephraim," the reason given is the same one we have just found in 1 Samuel and Numbers for *not* changing his mind: "For I am God and no mortal, the Holy One in your midst" (Hos. 11:9). Now, the writers of the Old Testament were by no means stupid. They knew what they were saying and knew what other traditions had said. I believe the tensions in the way God is represented in Exodus 32–34 ought to be lived with rather than smoothed out, for they are likely to get us closer to the true God than any simple, easily understood picture. This is one example of the tensions that run throughout this section. But the burden of the evidence is that what is consistent about God is the intention to save, so that any reason at all may be enough for God to decide to avert an act of judgment.

It is Moses' conviction that this is the true character of God, and that makes him bold enough to contradict God's decision to judge Israel. Moses must have been convinced that he was in fact on God's side when he reminded him of what is reasonable and in keeping with God's reputation

---

16. Terence E. Fretheim, "The Repentance of God," 52.

and character. Other Israelites also understood so well their utter dependence on the grace of God that some of them added this term *hinnahem* to their formulations of the great confession of faith that appears near the end of this section of Exodus, in 34:6-7. The Exodus form is "Yahweh, Yahweh, a God merciful and gracious, slow to anger, and abounding in steadfast love and faithfulness, keeping steadfast love for the thousandth generation, forgiving iniquity and transgression and sin, etc." Joel partially cites it in this way: "Return to the LORD, your God, for he is gracious and merciful, slow to anger, and abounding in steadfast love, and relents from punishing" (Joel 2:13). Those last three words from the NRSV are the identical words that the RSV translates "repent of evil" in Exodus 32:12. Jonah alludes to the same confession in his own way in 4:2 (NRSV): "O LORD! Is not this what I said while I was still in my own country? That is why I fled to Tarshish at the beginning; for I knew that you are a gracious God and merciful, slow to anger, and abounding in steadfast love, and ready to relent from punishing." These two formulations strengthen the already powerful group of words describing God's grace and mercy by insisting that God is even ready to reverse his own decisions in order to avoid judgment.

Thus Israel seems to insist on a changeable God, and Christians have never been comfortable with that. "Immortal, invisible, God only wise," the hymn begins and, eventually, in the third verse, comes to this, "We blossom and flourish as leaves on the tree, and wither and perish — but nought changeth thee." Can we handle the idea of a God who changes his mind — and do we need to? Isn't there something wrong about this?

Taking passages such as this more literally than has been done before, in the belief that this is to take them more seriously, is related to twentieth-century Christianity's willingness to speak of a God who suffers, thus of a God who is not unmoved, implacable, without feeling, but who is truly affected by what happens on earth.[17] Of course, the Old Testament speaks of God that way throughout, but its language has from early Judaism to this day been explained away as poetry or anthropomorphism, either of which needs to be interpreted — rationalized. Maybe twentieth-century Christianity is wrong, but at this point I believe that although speaking of

17. For the Old Testament evidence, Terence E. Fretheim, *The Suffering of God: An Old Testament Perspective* (Philadelphia: Fortress, 1984). For an analysis of two twentieth-century theologians, Ronald Goetz, "Karl Barth, Jürgen Moltmann and the Theopaschite Revolution" in *Festschrift: A Tribute to Dr. William Hordern,* ed. W. Freitag (Saskatoon: University of Saskatchewan, 1985): 17-28.

God as truly being affected by what we do and as being willing to change in response to us may remove us a step from parts of our creeds, it brings us closer to the God of Scripture.

Surely we must admit that the conviction (often poorly integrated with the rest of our theology) that God really does respond to us, which means God is willing to change, is the essential foundation for the belief that prayers of petition and intercession are possible. For if God does not truly let our prayers affect him, what are we doing? The idea didn't fit Calvin's theology very well, but we noticed that in his comments on Exodus 32 he cautiously allowed for it. Karl Barth was far less cautious, as he found petition to be the single element distinguishing prayer from other forms of worship. He concluded,

> It is thus a form of his sovereignty, and therefore of his immutable vitality that He is willing not merely to hear but to hearken to the prayer of faith and that He not only permits to faith the prayer which expects an answer but has positively commanded it. The living and genuinely immutable God is not an irresistible fate before which man can only keep silence, passively awaiting and accepting the benefits or blows which it ordains.[18]

Such affirmations of the changeability of God, even of God's vulnerability to the will of human beings, at first sound like a serious weakening of our belief in the sovereignty of God, and certainly it is not easy to combine all that the Scripture says of God in this regard into a theological formulation of our own. Taking these parts of the Old Testament with the utmost seriousness does not call for a weakening but for a refinement of our statements about sovereignty. Fretheim, for example, says this: ". . . not to be able genuinely to respond or interact, not to be open and vulnerable, or refusing to change are in fact signs of imperfection. In all of this, it is important to say that God changes *as God,* not as the creatures"[19] — that is, it is important to keep reminding ourselves that even the word "change" is a metaphor, reflecting only imperfectly the true nature of God.

Karl Barth made a similarly strong statement about changeability and sovereignty:

---

18. Karl Barth, *Church Dogmatics,* vol. II.1, *The Doctrine of God* (Edinburgh: T. & T. Clark, 1957): 511; cf. *CD,* vol. III.3, *The Doctrine of Creation,* 285.
19. Terence E. Fretheim, "The Repentance of God," 63.

It would be most unwise, then, to try to understand what the Bible says about God's repentance as if it were merely figurative. For what truth is denoted by the "figure" if we are not to deny that there is an underlying truth? Of course, in so far as this relationship rests on an attitude of God's, it is immutable in the sense that it is always and everywhere God's relationship to man, the being and essence of the One who loves in freedom. Yet it would not be a glorifying, but a blaspheming and finally a denial of God, to conceive of the being and essence of this self-consistent God as one which is, so to speak, self-limited to an inflexible immobility, thus depriving God of the capacity to alter His actions and attitudes as they are manifested in His revelation in concurrence or in sequence.[20]

Moses' insistence that God change was clearly based on his conviction as to what is unchangeable in God, namely his unwavering intention to save. Surely that, and that alone, can be the basis for our petitions, as well. According to the author of the story, Moses was not wrong. "The Lord changed his mind about the disaster that he planned to bring on his people" (Exod. 32:14).

20. Karl Barth, *CD*, vol. II.1, *The Doctrine of God*, 498. Also, "The special act of God in this new work [after the Fall] consists further in the fact that in these dealings God does not disdain to enter into a kind of partnership with man" (with reference to Gen. 18 and 32; Luke 18:1ff.) (*CD*, vol. II.1, *The Doctrine of God*, 507).

Silence and Weeping
before the Song

SAMUEL E. KARFF

"Not by facile theodicy, but through struggle at the very abyss may one claim a relation to the Holy Other more real and more personal than ever."

A day of sublime joy (Lev. 9) turned suddenly into a time of unspeakable sorrow (Lev. 10). The quick change of circumstance and mood is highlighted by the text's very spareness and its juxtapositions.

1. Divine Presence: Experienced Not Forced

The day began most auspiciously for Aaron, his wife Elisheva, and their four sons. The sanctuary had been completed and dedicated. Aaron and his sons were consecrated to the priesthood. They may now preside over the worship ceremonies in honor of the God of Israel. Aaron lifted up his hand and blessed the people. He conducted the ritual sacrifices — the sin offering, the burnt offering, and the offering of well-being. When Aaron stepped out of the sanctuary, he and Moses blessed the people.

> The glory of the LORD appeared to all the people. Then, fire came forth from before the LORD and consumed the burnt offering and the fat parts

on the altar, and all the people saw and shouted and fell on their faces. (Lev. 9:24)

What a dazzling moment of covenantal solidarity. The people had consecrated themselves, their sacred space, and their leaders to the service of God. In response, God's loving presence was felt, and, then, God's power became strikingly manifest: a heavenly flame came forth and consumed their offering.

While chapter 9 ends on a note of high spiritual resonance, the mood changes abruptly as we read of the deeds of Aaron's sons Nadab and Abbihu: "Each took his fire pan, put fire in it and laid incense in it and they offered before the LORD strange fire which he had not enjoined upon them. And fire came forth from the LORD and consumed them. Thus they died in the very presence of the LORD."

How quickly the scene changes. God sent the first heavenly flame to signal favor with the people and their leaders. God brings a second flame to destroy Aaron's two sons — punishment for their having offered "a strange fire" to the Lord.

In this tragic episode Aaron joins the biblical fellowship of parents disappointed by the acts of their offspring. He is preceded by Adam and Noah and Jacob (whose son violated his marital couch). He will be followed by the likes of Eli (1 Sam. 2:12): "and the children of Eli were evil doers who did not know the LORD." And Samuel (1 Sam. 8:3): "his sons did not follow his ways. They pursued personal gain."

Here, too, great opportunities for sacred stewardship are forfeited and a proud parent is reduced to bitter mourning. What actually happened? What was this strange fire? The text gives no explicit answers, but the classic rabbinic imagination does not fail us.

Some of the sages found an answer in chapter 10:9: "And the LORD spoke to Aaron saying 'wine and liquor do not drink, neither you nor your sons when you enter the tent of meeting lest you die'!" This injunction follows the report of Nadab and Abbihu's offense. So that must be it. Aaron's sons performed their priestly duties while intoxicated. Thus did they dishonor their vocation and profane the name of God.[1]

Many centuries later a Hasidic Rabbi Simcha Bunam of Przysucha expounded on this text. Rabbi Bunam notes that an early Midrash (Lev. Rabbah 12:3) elucidates this verse by citing another from Psalm 19: "The

---

1. Leviticus Rabbah 12:1.

precepts of the LORD are right, rejoicing the heart." This may mean that the divine Presence (*Shechina*) cannot appear in the midst of sadness; therefore, the priest is expected to preside at the altar in a spirit of exaltation and joy. If so, why would he be denied the benefit of wine? Does not wine beget joy ("wine rejoices a person's heart")?

The answer is that the priest who enters the Holy of Holies was expected to receive his feelings of pleasure and happiness from joy (the natural high) involved in fulfilling God's commandment. "The Torah of God should be the source of his inspiration and the wellspring of his joy. . . . Thus in Psalm 19 we read: 'The precepts of the Lord gladden the heart'! Nadab and Abbihu relied on external substances to produce their exaltation. That was their sin."[2]

For other exegetes the sin of Nadab and Abbihu was rank arrogance. In Exodus 24:1 we read of Moses' summons to the Mount of God. Aaron and Nadab and Abbihu and the seventy elders accompanied Moses only part of the way. One rabbi imagines Moses and Aaron walking ahead while Nadab and Abbihu followed. Nadab turned to his brother and said: "When will these two old fellows die and you and I will lead the generation?" The Holy One said to them: "Do not exult prematurely. Let us see who will bury whom."[3]

"Strange fire" may also have the aura of idolatry. If so, how bitterly ironic for Aaron to discover that the sons' transgression was in essence akin to his own "strange fire" at the foot of Sinai. Let us probe further the possible allusion to idolatry. In Leviticus 16:1 we are told that the two sons of Aaron "died when they drew too close to the presence of the Lord." To draw too close is to disregard the irreducible otherness of the sacred. Moses was warned against such impulsive disregard of boundaries at the burning bush. "Moses, Moses . . . do not come closer. Remove your sandals from your feet for the place in which you stand is holy ground" (Exod. 3:4-5).

The sin of Nadab and Abbihu stemmed from religious enthusiasm. Hunger for the sacred includes the urge to feel the nearness, the tangible presence of God. At times this translates into the urge to perform some act that will compellingly demonstrate both the presence and the power of the sacred. At times God may indulge this need for demonstration (Moses and Pharaoh, Elijah and the prophets of Baal), but such expectation must not become normative, nor may such testing be the ultimate ground for trust.

---

2. *Itturay Torah,* IV, ed. A. Y. Greenberg (Tel Aviv: Yavneh, 1976): 54.
3. Babylonian Talmud (Nezikin 52a).

On the day of the dedication of the tabernacle and the consecration of its priests Moses and Aaron hoped that God would be pleased — that the "glory of the LORD may appear" (Lev. 9:6). Elsewhere Rashi (Rabbi Solomon ben Isaac) interprets the appearance of God's glory as "the light of his countenance," the sense of God's loving presence. That Moses and Aaron hoped for and even dared to expect. But they did not impute to their offerings and blessings the power to force the dramatic self-disclosure of God in the fire that issued from heaven. That heavenly fire was an unexpected gift. So we read in Leviticus 9:23-24:

> And Moses and Aaron went into the tabernacle of the congregation and came out and blessed the people and the glory of the LORD appeared unto all the people and (then) there came a fire from before the LORD and consumed upon the altar the burnt offering and the fat which, when all the people saw, they shouted and fell on their faces.

What we have here is the difference between intimations of God's presence (which are, in part, reflections of our own openness — our seeing the world through the eyes of faith) and dramatic divine self-disclosure, which leaves little room for reasonable doubt ("And all the people saw and shouted and fell on their faces"). Such dramatic self-disclosure may not be willfully induced by human initiative. We may prepare ourselves for the intimations of God's love (the glory of the Lord), but the heavenly fire on the altar is an unexpected grace.

In this context we read of Nadab and Abbihu's "offering of strange fire which He commanded them not." They wanted to recreate or restage the appearance of the divine fire. They offered their fire in the expectation that it would be matched by another dramatic manifestation of God's power. At best they were overcome by a spirit of religious enthusiasm. At worst they were anxious to demonstrate their own sacred powers.

In either case they expected to force the hand of heaven by their act, which, in and of itself, is a religious posture closer to magic or idolatry than biblical faith. Nadab and Abbihu were as uncomfortable with a God who could not be seen and brought close at will as was their father's generation at the foot of Sinai. Drawing on the commentaries of Mendelsohn and S. R. Hirsch, Nehama Liebowitz observes:

> Their guilt . . . lay in man's desire to break through, as it were, to the Almighty and cleave to his Creator, not in accordance with the prescribed

ordinances but rather in conforming with the dictates of his own heart. The acceptance of the yoke of heaven . . . is here replaced by a religious ecstasy which is free from the trammels of normative religious discipline unrestrained and unsubservient to the Divine will.[4]

I suggest that Nadab and Abbihu's sin lay not so much in failing to follow prescribed norms nor in their cultic improvisation. Their religious enthusiasm, their strange fire, was an attempt to compel God's self-disclosure. They, spiritual leaders of the people, were themselves not reconciled to a God who is both hidden and revealed.

We must open ourselves to the sacred. Religious ritual is a time-hallowed means of fostering God-consciousness and drawing nearer to the Holy One. At times our performance of ritual (whether cultic sacrifice or prayer) is more fulfillment of covenant obligation than expression of love or awe deeply felt at the moment. Even so there will be times when we do pray with all our heart and yet feel we are speaking more to ourselves than to a God who is near.

Most precious are those moments of grace when God is "nearer to us than breathing." Memory of such moments sustains us in those other times and nourishes our hope for a recovery of the time of grace. The religious life demands that we pray and serve a God who at times seems distant or absent even as we cherish the memory and the moments of nearness.

Divine self-disclosure, peak experiences of the spirit, may not be created by force of will nor ought they be pursued calculatingly and obsessively. Rather, by *avodah* — by the service of worship and our stewardship and servanthood in the world we fulfill our covenant and open ourselves to intimations of God's presence.

The yearning for intimacy with the Divine is intrinsic to spiritual hunger, but respect for the otherness of the Sacred and an acceptance of the "I shall be as I shall be" quality of the Eternal One is the dominant hallmark of classical Judaism. Especially dangerous, therefore, is the religious leader's attempt to collapse the otherness of the divine either out of religious enthusiasm or the claim to be God's surrogate or successor on earth.

4. Quoted in N. Leibowitz, *Studies in Leviticus* (Jerusalem, 1980): 68.

2. Leadership Requires Accountability

Our text suggests that the very harshness of the punishment meted out to Nadab and Abbihu derived from their roles as religious leaders. Moses reminds Aaron of the divine declaration: "Through those near to me I show myself holy and assert my authority before all the people" (Lev. 10:2). Indeed, Moses was destined to have this principle apply to him when he struck the rock (Num. 20). In each case harsh punishment is linked to the special status of the transgressor.

The terse phrase, "Through those near to me I show myself holy," has resonances that echo through the centuries. What a burden to be cast as exemplar. There are times when all leaders yearn to be free of that special standard. How often do those who lapse seek shelter in their religion's assertion of human fallibility? Do not the transgressions of the leader confirm that we are all subject to temptation? Did not the rabbinic sages declare "the greater the man the greater the power of temptation with which he must contend"?

Yet, no one worthy of the mantle of leadership is permitted to be primarily the exemplar of weakness and spiritual fallibility. How devastating to the morale of the group, how destructive to their faith and faithfulness is the discovery that the priest has no clothes! Inescapably the claim to leadership requires special accountability.

To be sure, the people should temper judgment with compassion and empathy. Leaders should not be deprived of their claim to repentance and forgiveness, but it may be difficult if not impossible for the one who has egregiously faltered to regain the trust of those he has disappointed. Clergy who flagrantly violate a standard they have commended to their people may need to find their opportunities for self-renewal in another community. Those who repeatedly violate the standard may need to seek their renewal in another vocation.

3. A Comforter Should Not Increase Pain

The death of one's children is the harshest fate a parent can endure. Here on the very day when he and his sons were ordained for the priesthood, on the very day God's power and love was dramatically revealed, Aaron is confronted by an unbearable event. Nadab and Abbihu have been struck dead in the line of priestly duty.

And who is Aaron's comforter? The first words he hears after the shock of the events comes from Moses. Some comfort! Moses says in effect: "You see Aaron, that's what God meant when God said that through those near me I show myself holy."

No wonder Aaron responds with total silence. The shock of the events themselves are compounded by the stark insensitivity of his brother's words. It is the equivalent of a parent who has just watched her child run over by a car being told by a friend: "I warned you. That's what happens when you let your child play in the street!" Whatever the truth of the assertion, it remains incredibly ill-timed.

Periodically Scripture and rabbinic Midrash address the dynamics of comfort. It is told of Rabbi Yochanan ben Zakkai that when his son died disciples came to comfort him. Rabbi Eliezer reminded the grieving Yochanan that Adam also had a son who died yet Adam was consolable. Rabbi Yochanan retorted acerbically: "Is it not bad enough to nurse my own grief that you must remind me of the grieving Adam?" When Rabbi Yosi reminded Yochanan that Aaron had lost two sons and came to terms with his loss through the silence of resignation, Rabbi Yochanan made the same rejoinder.

After a string of unsuccessful comforters one disciple, Rabbi Elazar, told Yochanan this parable: "A man was entrusted by the king with some object. Each day the man tearfully agonized 'Woe unto me. When will I be relieved of this trust in peace?'" Then the teller of this parable drew his conclusion: "You, rabbi, had a son who was a diligent student of Torah and left this world without sin. You should be comforted that you have returned the one entrusted to you unblemished." These words proved comforting. Rabbi Yochanan turned to Rabbi Elazar and said: "You have comforted me in the manner persons should comfort one another."[5]

Some sages imagined that Moses' citation of God's words ("through those near to me I show myself holy") did comfort Aaron. He, their grieving father, was assured that his sons were among those close to and cherished by God. By their death they were privileged to sanctify the sanctuary. Their one lapse deprived them of their life but not of being accounted close to and cherished by their Creator. Moreover, God grieved over Aaron's loss even more than Aaron. Hence, it is claimed, Aaron was able to be silent and come to terms with God's decree.[6]

5. *Avot de Rabbi Natan,* trans. Judah Goldin (New Haven: Yale Univ. Press, 1955): 76-77.

6. Leviticus Rabbah 20:10.

For us Moses' words to Aaron could hardly dispel the pain of fresh loss, nor, for that matter, would Rabbi Elazar's words to Rabbi Yochanan comfort us. In all likelihood, at that moment of raw grief, no theodicy is efficacious. Better the comforter's silence and a warm embrace and that Aaron be permitted to cry out in pain. Better the comfort of empathic tears than any words of explanation.

More compelling is Andre Neher's understanding of Aaron's silence. It was the silence of one turned to stone, the mark of numbness, not acquiescence. Moses' words, like those of Job's comforters, deepened the estrangement between Aaron and God. "Here," writes Neher, "we put our finger on a biblical attitude which the example of Job illustrates in a remarkable manner, namely that man can accept God's silence but not that other men should speak in his place."[7]

Perhaps in the course of time Moses' efforts at theodicy could be helpful but not now. That is what another sage meant when he said: "Console him not in the hour when his dead lies before him."

4. Personal Need and Religious Responsibility

Moses' inadequacy as a comforter is searingly compounded by his subsequent remarks. He summoned levitical kin, Mishael and Elzaphan to "come forward and carry your kinsmen away from the foot of the sanctuary to a place outside the camp" (Lev. 10:4). Immediately thereafter (Lev. 10:6), Moses says to Aaron and his two surviving sons: "Do not bare your heads and do not rend your clothes lest you die and anger strike the whole community. But your kinsmen, all the house of Israel, shall bewail the burning that the LORD has wrought."

Moses then reminds Aaron and his sons (Lev. 10:7) why their need to mourn will, for the present, be denied them: "You must not go outside the entrance of the tent of meeting lest you die, for the LORD's anointing oil is upon you." And we are told: "They did as Moses had bidden." Moses expounds the price of being vested with sacred responsibilities. Aaron and his sons' grieving must be deferred until they have completed their priestly tasks within the tent of meeting.

These verses attained a clarifying power for me when I probed a personal anomaly. At each of my daughters' Bat Mitzvah ceremonies I was

7. Quoted by Pinchas Peli, *Jerusalem Post,* April 1, 1989, from Andre Neher.

both father and rabbi. When I passed the Torah to each and spoke words personal and liturgical my eyes misted and my voice cracked momentarily, but I remained generally in control. At a comparable ceremony for my sister's only son, in a congregation not my own, I was invited by the presiding rabbi to offer a word to my nephew. Then, in the midst of speaking, I faltered and broke into sobs.

Why the different response? On the occasion of my daughters' ceremonies I was also mindful of my responsibilities for conducting the worship service. At my nephew's Bar Mitzvah I had no such responsibilities. Then I spoke only as an uncle who could be permitted the full poignancy of the moment to overwhelm me. At my daughters' Bat Mitzvahs (like Aaron, though in a radically different mood) I was constrained by my priestly role in the congregation.

The conflict between personal need and public role is further illuminated by the plight of a colleague who battled a terminal illness yet insisted on performing his rabbinic duties virtually until he collapsed. To keep struggling to write, preach, even officiate at life cycle ceremonies was an act of sterling courage and an anguished effort to maintain a sense of rabbinic identity. Yet, on one occasion after he had presided at a funeral one of the mourners exclaimed: "It is not fair. I needed to mourn for my mother but I found myself mourning for my rabbi." At times, our acting vocationally out of personal need may impair our functioning as priest.

Are there times when the priest's personal needs should prevail? Was Aaron the high priest really expected to resume his priestly duties without taking into account the immediate death of his two sons? Can he truly respond to the pain in his heart unless he suspends his priestly duties?

5. Personal Need *over* Religious Responsibility?

From the text one would assume that Moses expected Aaron and his surviving sons to carry on as if nothing had happened. In this spirit of vocational priority Moses gives Aaron and his surviving sons Eliezer and Ithamar instructions concerning the meal offering, the breast offering, and the thigh offering (Lev. 10:12-18). It seems there will be sacred business as usual! The cultic service must go on. So what if Nadab and Abbihu have been consumed by fire and their scorched corpses just dragged from the altar! But must Aaron and his sons really act as if nothing untoward has befallen them?

With verse 16 we begin to discern a different answer to our query. When Moses diligently investigated the goat of the sin offerings he discovered that it had been burned by Aaron and his sons without their having partaken of its meat, yet the priestly consumption of the offering in the vicinity of the altar was part of the ritual of expiation for the sins of the community. Moses confronts Aaron and his sons angrily: "Why did you not eat the sin offering in the sacred area?" Now Aaron breaks his silence. "See this day they brought their sin offering and their burnt offering before the LORD and *such things have befallen me!* Had I eaten the sin offering today would the LORD have approved?" (Lev. 10:19).

For the first time Aaron permits the tragic "things that have befallen" him to shape his response. Has he now yielded to the impulses of his heart and permitted his personal grief to shape his priestly behavior? Or is Aaron simply following a divine injunction to refrain from that particular ritual while in a state of mourning?

Jewish commentators over the centuries have taken each point of view. The Sifra expounds Aaron's behavior in legal terms. The death of Aaron's sons took place on the first day of the month. Aaron did carry out his priestly duties that day. Three goats were brought as sin offerings: the goat of the people (Lev. 9:15) and the goat offered by Nachshon, the chieftain of Judah (Num. 7:16), and the sin offering regularly brought on the first day of the month. Aaron and his sons did partake of the meat of the first two offerings because he considered them special sacrifices connected with his ordination, which he should consume even in a state of fresh grief. But Aaron held that a general rule that priests should not eat sacrificial meat during mourning applied only to the third goat. This new moon sacrifice was not extraordinary but part of a monthly ritual that should be suspended when the priest is in mourning.

According to this view God's covenant law (which the rabbis called *halachah*) provided Aaron and his sons a warrant for acting differently even as officiating priests when in a state of mourning. Moses, in his anger over a supposed infraction of divine law, actually overlooked or forgot or misinterpreted the law. To Moses' credit he acknowledged his error. When Moses heard a proper legal explanation he approved.[8]

Alternately Jewish commentators have viewed Aaron's rejoinder to Moses not as a legal justification of his behavior but as a welling up of the promptings of his heart, which he believed would receive divine under-

8. Babylonian Talmud (Zevachim 101a).

standing and favor. Rashbam (Rabbi Samuel ben Meir) imagines Aaron saying: "Only today did we make our dedication offerings which were marred by a great personal tragedy and (now that) there have befallen me such things as these how can I partake of the most holy sin offering when we cannot bring to the act a joyful heart?"[9]

Mendelsohn's commentary (Biur) has Aaron say, "If I restrained myself and did not weep in order to show publicly my acceptance of divine judgment, would it be well pleasing in the sight of the Lord to partake of the sin offering in joy while my heart is full of grief and sorrow?"[10]

Aaron's grief is finally validated and deemed an appropriate ground for modifying his behavior even in the midst of his priestly duties. Thus is our biblical passage permitted to reflect a tension between the officiant's vocational duty and deep personal need. God is cast as a sympathetic observer of that struggle.

Actually, the Torah itself makes a distinction between the high priest, who must not grieve publicly even for a departed son (Lev. 21:10-12), and regular priests like Aaron's sons. The latter may grieve publicly for close relatives, including a deceased brother (Lev. 21:1f). But what if the death occurs in the midst of their religious duties?

Rabbinic law created in the category of *aninut,* a state of mourning between the occurrence of the death and burial rites. During that period regular priests (Aaron's sons) are required to mourn for close relatives even if the news reaches them in the midst of their official duties. Even if they do not leave the sanctuary, they stop their sacred service. One commentator, Rabad (Abraham ben David of Posquieres), suggests that since the priest is obligated to mourn he will feel impelled, even against his will, to leave the sanctuary and become ritually unclean through contact with the dead relatives.[11]

As for all other Jews, rabbinic law provides that during the period between the death of a loved one and the burial, one is exempt from virtually all religious duties. "One whose dead relatives lie before him is exempt from the recitation of the Shema, and from prayer and from tefillin (the prayerboxes used in morning devotion) and from all precepts laid down in the Torah" (16). In a period of fresh grief a person is relieved of all duties.

9. Quoted in N. Leibowitz, *Studies in Leviticus,* 73-74.
10. Quoted in N. Leibowitz, *Studies in Leviticus,* 74.
11. See Moses Maimonides, *Mishneh Torah,* book 2, chapter 2, Halachah 6, 7.

6. God Not Offended by a Heavy Heart

"And Aaron was silent." In the immediacy of a monumental loss Aaron's silence could hardly betoken the inner peace that comes from reconciliation to the ways of God. Wisely, rabbinic tradition regards mourning as a *mitzvah,* a religious duty. Only by stepping aside from the normal rhythms of life, only by temporarily modifying one's life routine, only by pausing to grieve, anguish, doubt, and struggle anew for one's covenant faithfulness can healing come.

Even if Aaron acknowledged instantly that his sons died because they offered strange fire that God had not commanded, he might still not be ready to offer God the silence of acceptance. One must be given the freedom to cry and lament before such silence. Only the silence of a paralyzing numbness can precede the outpouring of the soul that may, in turn, yield to the silence of acceptance. Judged by the evidence of Jeremiah's confessions or Job's plaint, the God of Israel is not offended by the outpouring of a heavy heart. And one, in turn, discovers that not by facile theodicy but through struggle at the very edge of the abyss may one reclaim a relation to the Holy Other more real and more personal than ever.

Rabbi Lipman once spoke these words to Rabbi Mendel of Kotsk in the name of his father-in-law: "Our sages regard as a pinnacle of piety Aaron's silence upon hearing of the death of his sons Nadab and Abbihu . . . but greater is that virtue attributed to King David who said: 'You have turned my mourning into dancing. You have put off my sackcloth and girded me with gladness in order that I may sing praises to You and not be silent' (Ps. 30:11f). Even in the depth of his sorrow David continued to sing unto God and was not silent." "Such is wonderful," said the Rabbi of Kotsk.

But for most of us who have experienced life's darkest side, the transition from silence to song is not gained save by taking the path of grief and mourning. The author of Psalm 30 (as I translate him) also experienced that long dark night before the sun: "Weeping (must) tarry for the night and (only) then joy may come in the morning."

The Way of Torah:
Escape from Egypt

FREDRICK C. HOLMGREN

*One cannot "approach the divine by reaching
beyond the human." (Martin Buber)*

"I Am Holy" — "Be Holy" (Lev. 19:2)

Divine Holiness: Above and Beyond

God is the Incomparable One who stands ever beyond the reach of human
categories — continually escaping the capturing net cast by religious thinkers
and institutions. In the Hebrew Bible, this "beyond" aspect of God is
sometimes related to God's *holiness* (e.g., Isa. 40:25; 1 Sam. 2:2; Ps. 102:19)
whose basic meaning in Hebrew is probably "separation." Often when we
think about the *holy* God, the picture that captures the mind is that of the
Awesome Other — a picture whose background colors are sternness,
demand, and threat. The above view may be one aspect of holiness, but it is
not the whole. A different image of the *holy* God emerges from other passages
of Scripture, as may be seen in the following paragraphs.

I am thankful to Leanne L. Motsenbocker, former tutor in Hebrew Bible at North Park
Theological Seminary, for her assistance in the preparation of this exposition.

117

Divine Holiness: Near and Humane

The main and continuing message of biblical literature is of a God who
seeks relationship with the people divinely created. God is the God who
dwells "in the high and holy place *and* also with those who are contrite
and humble in spirit" (Isa. 57:15). The great prophet of the Exile finds
comfort and hope in the Holy One of Israel (e.g., Isa. 43:3), and Hosea
underscores God's otherness ("I am God and no mortal, the Holy One in
your midst") in order to emphasize his compassion for Israel even in the
face of high-handed sinfulness (Hos. 11:9). Further, it is the three times
holy God who responds to Isaiah with forgiveness rather than threat (Isa.
5:16), and it is the temple where Yahweh "dwells" that is called a "holy
place"; it is at this "holy place" that people expect God to hear their prayers
and to respond with help (e.g., Ps. 20:2; RSV: "sanctuary").

The holy God does not live in aloof transcendence — letting human
beings lie in the hard bed they have made for themselves. Although distance
and otherness are important aspects of the divine holiness, the *holy* God is
never so transcendent as to cease being Immanuel, the God who is with
and for us.

"I Am the LORD Your God"

The above phrase, or one similar to it, occurs about sixteen times in
Leviticus 19.[1] At first glance, the repetition of this declaration seems to
emphasize that God is the transcendent ruler who demands that Israel
submit to divine authority. However, the expression, "I am the LORD your
God," is not meant to overwhelm Israel with divine majesty; rather, it is
by means of this announcement that Israel's Rescuer is identified, as may
be seen in verse 36: "I am the LORD your God, *who brought you out of
the land of Egypt* . . . I am the LORD." The oft repeated expressions "I am
the LORD" or "I am the LORD your God" are, no doubt, only short forms
of this longer one occurring in verse 36. This LORD is the God who saw
the oppressive acts of the Egyptians, heard the cries of those caught in the
grasp of unfeeling oppressors — who "knew" their condition (Exod. 2:21-
25). God is the compassionate one who has called the Israelites to be
partners in creating a society that will reflect divine (com)passion for

---

1. See: vv. 2, 3, 4, 10, 12, 14, 16, 18, 25, 28, 30, 31, 32, 34, 36, and 37.

people. God's teachings provide room for everyone to live, expand, and find fulfillment. The "laws" are not burdensome or too restrictive — except for those who want to "edge ahead" by taking advantage of other members of the community. Israel is called upon to obey God's teachings not so much to show subservience to divine authority as to emulate the kindness that God displayed to the Israelite community in the Exodus from Egypt.

A Holy Community: Saying No and Yes

The initial verses of Leviticus 19 call the community to be the holy people of the holy God. We do not understand today all of what it meant for the Israelites to be a part of a holy community because some parts of this chapter are marked by great age and speak of customs and understandings that, for most people today, are lost in history (e.g., Lev.19:19).[2] Generally, however, these verses paint a clear picture of what a holy society is like when it comes to *human relationships*. When Leviticus 19 speaks of the *holy* God, it is calling attention to God's desire to form *God's kind* of community — a holy community where everyone has a chance at life.

As we read these verses that describe a holy community, we become aware that to be holy means saying a firm no — separating oneself from an all-too-common way of living. The following verses, for example, summon people to reject attitudes and actions that are ruinous to community wholeness (Lev. 19:11-18, 20, 27, 33, 35):

> Stealing, lying, cheating, oppression, insensitivity;
> Making fun of the handicapped (the blind and deaf);
> Playing favorites in matters of judgment;
> Spreading rumors, treasuring secret, avenging anger;
> Sending one's daughter into prostitution;
> Taking advantage of a vulnerable woman slave;
> Oppressing a foreigner.

---

2. For an understanding of ancient customs that appear irrelevant to people today, see Mary Douglas' discussion on "The Abominations of Leviticus" in *Purity and Danger* (London: Penguin, 1970): 41-57. Nicholas Wolterstorff provides a summary of her views in "Liturgy, Justice, and Holiness," *The Reformed Journal* 39 (Dec. 1989): 15-18.

On the other hand, belonging to a holy community means saying a committed yes — separating oneself to a community where people live as children in the family of God (1 Pet. 1:13-16). The above admonitions to reject ruinous acts *imply* positive deeds that make for a shalom community (for example, instead of being a rumor-bearer, speak well of people). The following texts, however, mention *explicitly* positive actions to which people should commit themselves (Lev. 19:3, 10, 15, 30, 32, 36):

> Honoring of parents and the aged;
> Reverence for the sabbath and the temple;
> Generosity toward the poor and foreigners;
> The establishing of justice in all areas of life.

This positive stance within the community is memorably summarized in two statements (Lev. 19:18, 34):

> You shall not take vengeance or bear a grudge against any of your people, but you shall love your neighbor as yourself. The alien who resides with you shall be to you as the citizen among you; you shall love the alien as yourself.

At center, Leviticus 19 is a summons of Israel to humane, kind acts. These deeds of justice, rather than the making of god-images (Lev. 19:4), give true witness to the nature of Israel's God. Abraham Heschel's words provide beautiful commentary:

> In a sacred deed, we echo God's suppressed chant; in loving we intone God's unfinished song. *No image of the Supreme may be fashioned, save one: our own life as an image of His will.* Man formed in His likeness, was made to imitate His ways of mercy. He has delegated to man the power to act in His stead. We represent Him in relieving affliction, in granting joy.[3]

In short, Leviticus 19 declares: *Be* the image of God in this world by acting compassionately toward others.

---

3. A. J. Heschel, *God in Search of Man* (New York: Harper Torchbooks, 1966): 290. Emphasis mine.

Leviticus 19: A Chance at Life for Everyone

For the reader who is familiar with the books of Exodus, Deuteronomy, and the prophets, many teachings in Leviticus, which speak of human relationships, are not new.[4] Although the teaching of this chapter may be a well-trod path, much of its teaching confronts real-life interrelationships where people find happiness, fulfillment, or hurt. The seeming prosaic aspect of this chapter may cause the reader to miss its importance. The teaching does not appear to meet us on the "spiritual" level; it seems to lack theological depth and spiritual uplift! We are impatient with such teaching ("yes, yes, we know all of that"). We want to deal with deeper, more important matters — *we want to know God at a personal, spiritual level.*

The message of the Law and the prophets, however, remind us that the teaching of Leviticus 19 stands at the center of divine concern. With sunshine clarity, this concern is set forth in an oracle recorded in Jeremiah. Concerning King Josiah, whose rule was characterized by justice and righteousness, God declares: "He judged the cause of the poor and needy; then it was well. *Is not this to know me?* says the LORD" (Jer. 22:15-16). Although "meeting" with God may be highly personal, Martin Buber is right in observing that God reveals himself (and is known) best in this world, by what happens *between* people.

To split off the personal, spiritual life from practical, daily relationships is a common temptation for the religious community. This compartmental thinking seduced some people in ancient Israel (see, e.g., Amos 4:1-5), and it has not lost its allure for contemporary religious institutions. True faith according to the Law and the prophets is to reflect God's "humanity" to the world.

Karl Barth has rightly observed: "One cannot speak of God simply by speaking of man in a *loud* voice."[5] But a counterstatement is also true: When one says "humankind" *with compassion,* one speaks most truly of the God of the Bible. In full agreement with the teaching of Sinai and the

---

4. In Leviticus 19, for example, one finds references or allusions to the Ten Commandments: vv. 3, 4, 11, 12, 16, 29, 36. Some verses refer to more than one of the Commandments. With regard to similar teachings in the New Testament, see: Matt. 20:8; 1 Tim. 5:1-2; 1 Pet. 1:15; James 3:1-10, 4:11; Matt. 18:15; Rom. 13:8-10; Gal. 5:14-15; James 2:8; Mark 12:28-31.

5. Karl Barth, *The Word of God and the Word of Man* (New York: Harper Torchbooks, 1957): 196. Emphasis mine.

Jewish tradition, Jesus rejects a sharp separation of the divine sphere from that of the human. In response to the question as to which commandment is the "first of all," Jesus replies:

> The first is "Hear, O Israel: The Lord our God, the Lord is one; and you shall love the Lord your God with all your heart, and with all your soul, and with all your mind, and with all your strength." The second is, "You shall love your neighbor as yourself." There is no other commandment greater than these. (Mark 12:28-31)

Martin Buber's characterization of the central teaching of Hasidic Judaism is another way of expressing the same truth: "Man cannot approach the divine by reaching beyond the human."[6]

Leviticus: Be Holy; Matthew: Be Perfect

As already mentioned, the initial words of Leviticus 19 are a call to the Israelite community to be holy: "You shall be holy, for I the LORD your God am holy." With regard to human relationships, this called-for holiness means *separation from* the "me first and foremost" attitude of the privileged, but it means also *separation to* (a commitment to) a compassionate, understanding treatment of other members of society.

Words ascribed to Jesus carry a message similar to that of Leviticus 19, namely: "You, therefore, must be perfect, as your heavenly Father is perfect" (Matt. 5:48). This verse concludes a long passage that summons the disciples to create loving, reconciling, compassionate relationships. This call to be "perfect" seems to have the meaning: be perfect (i.e., fully committed) in love to others. The Revised English Bible (1989) represents this view with its translation: "There must be no limit to your goodness, as your heavenly Father's goodness knows no bounds." The parallel passage in Luke 6:36 points toward such an interpretation. Luke substitutes *merciful* for *perfect:* "Be ye therefore merciful, as your Father is merciful." Whether the call is to be "holy" or to be "perfect," the expectation is basically the same: one committed to divine teaching who communicates by word and deed the humanness of God.

6. This statement comes from Martin Buber, but I am unable to find its source.

Torah-Teaching: Do Not Imitate Egypt

The enslavement of the Hebrews in Egypt is a continuing memory in the Hebrew Bible.[7] The giving of the Law on Mt. Sinai is set in the context of Israel's deliverance from Egyptian slavery. God identifies himself to the Israelites: "I am the LORD your God who brought you out of Egypt." This divine declaration is considered the first commandment (teaching) in the Jewish tradition. The God who delivered the Hebrews out of slavery gave to them a law whose teachings, unlike those of Egypt, bestowed life on *all* members of society. It is within the context of Israel's slavery experience in Egypt that we are to understand God's word addressed to her through Moses in Leviticus 18–19. See, for example, Leviticus 18:3-5:

> You shall not do as they do in the land of Egypt, where you lived. . . . You shall not follow their statues. My ordinances you shall observe and my statues you shall keep, following them: I am the LORD your God [who brought you out of the land of Egypt. See Lev. 19:36]. You shall keep my statues and my ordinances; by doing so one shall live: I am the LORD.

However, it is not so easy to walk away from oppressive rule and order one's life in a new way. Although abusive rule is painful to endure, it invades the thought and feeling centers of the victim and presses there its malevolent mark. The victims begin to accept their treatment as something they must accept, that "that's the way life is." The real imprisonment of Israel in the land of Egypt, according to Rabbi Hanokh, was not that the Israelites were forced by the Pharaoh to remain there as slaves. No! Rather, it was their acceptance of the Egyptian way of life; they learned to "endure" it. They became accustomed to Egypt as they would become accustomed to Canaan.[8] Apparently, however, there was not only a fear that the Israelites would *endure* the oppressive rule of Canaan (as they had Egypt) but that they would actually *imitate* the Egyptian and Canaanite

---

7. Negative references to Egypt in this paper reflect the Israelite memory of a time of slavery in Egypt. It is not, of course, a blanket condemnation of all Egyptian culture and civilization. Many peoples today have similar memories of times of oppression by other countries as well as by secular and religious institutions.

8. See Martin Buber, *Tales of the Hasidim: Later Masters* (New York: Schocken, 1948): 315: "Rabbi Hanokh said: 'The real exile of Israel in Egypt was that they learned to endure it.' "

way of life. Thus Moses is directed to warn the Israelites: "You shall *not do* as they do in the land of Egypt, where you lived, and you shall *not do* as they do in the land of Canaan . . ." (Lev. 18:3).

The Egyptian Way of Life: Israelized, Americanized

On the one hand, the Israelites desperately wanted liberation from the hard life of slavery, which each day meant heavy work, mistreatment, lack of freedom; but, on the other hand, they enslaved themselves unconsciously by allowing Egyptian thought patterns to enter their own way of thinking. Some Israelites, like children who have been abused by adults, imitated the one who had abused them and acted as Egyptians toward other Israelites. God brought the Israelites out of Egypt, but "Egypt" still imprisoned the Israelites from within. What remained to be done was to take Egypt out of the Israelites — a more difficult task than the one accomplished by Moses and one never fully completed.

Egypt hung on and hung in. In the whole range of Israelite history, Egypt was present as a resilient virus that was never completely knocked out by Torah. Nehemiah, for example, tells of acts of oppression in the post-exilic period when the powerful rich took advantage of the poor in Israel forcing an "outcry" from the victims (Neh. 5:6) — an outcry not unlike that which escaped the lips of the Israelites when they suffered in the "smelting furnace" of Egyptian oppression (Exod. 2:23; cf. Deut. 4:20). And the story continues. Within the American society this dehumanizing virus is still alive — and "healthy."

Leviticus 19: Escape Route from "Egypt"

Leviticus 19 summons us to reject Egypt by refusing to oppress others (e.g., Lev. 19:13-15) and by a firm resolve to create a community where people can count on impartial justice and humane action (e.g., Lev. 19:15-18). But the Egypt within is firmly entrenched and difficult to cast out; it is an influential force whose strength with the passage of time seems never to diminish. We learn to endure injustice in our communities and institutions — become accustomed to the use and abuse of people — and, sometimes, become ourselves abusers. Even religious institutions that honor the Gospel and Torah become accustomed to a society in which the strong, the influential, and the privileged have their way. The Egypt within us covers the eye to tragedy and the ear from the cry.

Can we escape Egypt? Or, control Egypt? A reading of Scripture can create a pessimistic response. Surely, there would not be such a strong and continuing rebuke of inhumane behavior in Scripture if such conduct were only a now-and-then appearance. Undoubtedly the community standing behind Leviticus 19 is blotched with intentional and unintentional evil. The "you shall" and "you shall not" teaching of the text presupposes that people in this community are not doing what they should be doing and, correspondingly, committing acts that should not be done.

Yet, within the text there appears hope for change; the appeals to do justice and to turn away from unrighteous acts carry within them the assumption that some people will respond. Further, although the history of Israel offers many examples of unfeeling, even cruel behavior, this same history makes us aware that an impressive number of people in Israelite society did, in fact, cast off Egypt by responding positively to the teaching of Torah and the proclamation of the prophets. How else does one explain the preservation of this literature as holy Scripture. When it is remembered that this literature includes warnings and sharp criticism of Israelite society, one can only conclude that it was a remarkably self-critical, Torah-faithful people who selected such a literature to be its holy guide to life!

Doing Love

In its emphasis on right human relationships, Leviticus is calling upon the Israelites to share with others that which they so much longed for but rarely found in the fire of Egyptian oppression (Deut. 4:20), that is, a compassion that expresses itself in humane action. Sharing such practical love, especially with the vulnerable members of society, offers the only certain escape route from Egypt.

Love is both an emotion and an act, but in the biblical tradition the emphasis is on *acting*. Loving God means *doing* God's commandments (Deut. 6:4-9). The words of Jesus in John reflect this same understanding: "If you love me, keep my commandments." In Leviticus 19:18 and 34, set in the midst of teachings that call for humane acts, the emphasis is not different. The Hebrew Bible does not so much expect one *to build up feelings of love* toward other people as to do the loving *act* that seeks the good of the other person (see, e.g., Deut. 22:1-4; Prov. 25:21).

Love the Insider and the Outsider

The NRSV reflects a traditional translation of Leviticus 19:18: "You shall not take vengeance or bear any grudge against any of *your people,* but you shall *love your neighbor as yourself:* I am the LORD." This passage, along with Deuteronomy 6:4, is quoted by Jesus and is understood to be a summary of the Torah (Mark 12:28-31 and parallels; see also James 2:8). This dual teaching is reflected also in the Jewish tradition (e.g., in the Teaching of the Twelve Patriarchs: Test. Iss. 5:2 and Test. Dan. 5:3). The neighbor in Leviticus 19:18 is no doubt the Israelite neighbor — the insider. However, in Leviticus 19:34, another passage occurs that has to do with the outsider:[9]

> When an *alien* resides with you in your land, you shall not oppress the *alien.* The *alien* who resides with you shall be to you as the citizen among you, and *you shall love the alien as yourself;* for you were *aliens* in the land of Egypt: I am the LORD your God.

A remarkable passage! An immigrant in the land of Israel is to be treated as if a native Israelite: "You shall love the alien as yourself." Quite other was Israel's experience in Egypt; there she knew what it was to be treated as an outsider, with few rights and little respect. In this passage and elsewhere, she is called upon to remember her experience — her pain, her hopes — and to break down the wall that separates insider and outsider (Exod. 22:21; 23:9; Deut. 10:18-19). Both the insider (the Israelite neighbor) and the outsider (the immigrant) are to be treated as one would like oneself to be treated.

Sometimes it is thought that Leviticus 19:18 and 34 ("you shall love your neighbor/the alien as yourself") point toward a theology of self-love. To speak of a "theology of self-love," however, is to read too much into these words. It is better to say that these texts build on the common wisdom of "self-concern." Such concern is affirmed in the Hebrew Scriptures (especially in the wisdom tradition) and in Jewish writings.[10] The declara-

---

9. The linking of the summary of the law with the parable of the Good Samaritan in Luke 10:23-37 implies that for him the neighbor includes both the outsider and the insider.

10. See, e.g., the Babylonian Talmud (Abot I, 14), which records the words of Hillel: "If I am not for myself, who is then for me? If I am only for myself, who am I? And if not now, then when?"

tion, "you shall love your neighbor/the alien as yourself," assumes that there is a "kinship" of humanity existing between the neighbor/alien and the self; the concerns of the one are also the concerns of the other. Both we and the neighbor/alien are concerned about preserving life, receiving help, finding acceptance, and realizing fulfillment. Leviticus 19:34 concludes with, "you were aliens in the land of Egypt," which reminds Israel of her concerns in Egypt — how she longed to be treated with respect and compassion. These self-concerns are to be the measure of her treatment of the alien.

Martin Buber's translation of Leviticus 19:18 and 34 points in the direction of the view expressed above: "Be loving to your fellow man [insider and outsider], as to one who is just like you."[11] The two texts in Leviticus 19 do not have in view a generalized human being — a member of humanity. Rather the person to which this teaching refers is the one we *meet* daily at work, in the neighborhood, or on the street — who emerges from the blur of humankind and confronts us as an individual with special facial features, voice, and character. *This* person is not an It to be used and abused but is a Thou who, "just like you," is created by God and wants to live, feel secure, receive help, and find fulfillment.

The Golden Rule

Leviticus 19:18 and 34, as many have observed, are, in fact, alternate statements of the so-called Golden Rule that finds expression in both the Jewish and Christian traditions. Hillel, a great Jewish teacher who was a contemporary of Jesus, said: "That which you hate, do not do to your neighbor. This is the whole of the Torah, everything else is just explanation. So go and learn!" (B.T., Sab. 31a; cf. Tobit 4:15). Another statement of this same teaching is recorded in the New Testament: "In everything do to others as you would have them do to you; for this is the law and the prophets" (Matt. 7:12; but see also B.T. Aboth 2:15 and 4:15). Although

11. Quoted by Bernard Bamberger in *The Torah: A Modern Commentary,* ed. Gunther Plaut (New York: Union of American Hebrew Congregations, 1981): 893. Whether this translation represents the original sense of the text is debated. Nevertheless, this basic *understanding* of the text is reflected already in early Jewish writings — even if the full interpretation is not exactly that of Buber's. See further N. Leibowitz, *Studies in Vayikra [Leviticus]* (Jerusalem, 1980): 194-198, and Reinhard Heudecker, "Lev 19,18 in Jewish Interpretation," *Biblica* 73 (1992): 496-517.

the New Testament formulation of the rule is positively stated, the negative statement of the rule appears to have been widely used in early Christianity.[12] We are fortunate in having both the negative and positive statement of the rule because, while they teach the same truth, they create different images in the mind (i.e., those actions that hurt us as well as those that make us happy). But either way, this rule reminds us that with regard to the treatment of other people, *self-awareness is an important aspect of divine guidance!*

Nevertheless, Leviticus 19:18 and 34 are hard words just because one is called to see the other as one like oneself. Frequently our acts toward others reflect little awareness of who we are or what we expect of others; rather, they are unexamined, thoughtless actions that rise out of group-think.

But there *are* times of surprise when people have heart and the neighbor/stranger is seen to be a feeling human being as we are. In these humane responses to others we become, as Abraham Heschel likes to say, "reminders" of the holy God of the Bible, the one who has created us and taught us how to be truly human. A story out of the Jewish hasidic tradition speaks the final word:

> An old rabbi [the Baal Shem-Tov] once asked his students how one could recognize the time when night ends and day begins. "Is it when, from a great distance, you can tell a dog from a sheep?" one student asked. "No," said the rabbi. "Is it when, from a great distance, you can tell a date palm from a fig tree?" another student asked. "No," said the rabbi. "Then when is it?" the students asked. "It is when you look into the face of any human creature and see your brother or your sister there. Until then, night is still with us."[13]

---

12. For a listing of passages in early Christian literature, see Albrecht Dihle, *Die Goldene Regel* (Göttingen: Vandenhoeck & Ruprecht, 1962): 106-107.

13. Quoted by Dorothee Sölle, "Love Your Neighbor as Yourself" in *The Strength of the Weak: Toward a Christian Feminist Identity* (Philadelphia: Westminster, 1984): 41.

"Would That All Were Prophets!"

CARROLL STUHLMUELLER, C.P.

"Prophecy is not a prerogative of any institution nor is it bestowed only in a sacred place."

Moses' response to Joshua, son of Nun, "Would that all the LORD's people were prophets!" (Num. 11:29) is "a passage of enormous significance for our understanding of the outward manifestations of prophecy."[1] Moses' statement is at once vague and clear! Vague, because it hardly settled Joshua's complaint against Eldad and Medad. These two men suddenly began to prophesy in the camp, even though "they had not gone out to the tent" of meeting when the LORD "took some of the spirit that was on [Moses] and put it on the seventy elders," ordaining them as elders and enabling them to prophesy (Num. 11:25-26). Moses' words are equally clear, declaring for God's freedom in bestowing the spirit of prophecy, clear enough to sound a strong prophetic call into centuries of theological development and pastoral ministry. Glen Levandowski caught the kaleidoscopic variations in this passage of Numbers 11:29,

---

An earlier draft of this chapter constituted the basic exegetical document for the III Plenary Assembly of the World Catholic Federation for the Biblical Apostolate, Bangalore, India, 12-24 August 1984. Cf. *God's Prophetic People* (ed. Robert J. Delaney; WCFBA General Secretariat, Postfach 601, 7000 Stuttgart 1, Germany), pp. 249-61.

    1. John F. A. Sawyer, *Prophecy and the Prophets of the Old Testament* (Oxford: Oxford University Press, 1987): 8.

Moses's "would that" is not exactly a prayer, nor really a promise, nor a proposal, not a softened imperative. [It is] sustaining, provocative, and impelling, forward-looking, at once athirst and quenching.[2]

Not only Moses' blunt and rallying reply to Joshua, but the entire chapter 11 of Numbers reaches into many moments of Israelite history. This biblical text, as a result, has become ensnarled in problems of transmission and interpretation. It reflects many divergent moments of prophecy, struggling against religious and civil leadership, or at other times cooperating with it and actually forming an integral part of it. To appreciate the rich and decisive teaching in Numbers 11, we will reflect: first, upon preliminary aspects in our approach to prophecy, important for contextualizing this chapter of Numbers and for pastoral situations today; and second, more specifically upon the relation of this passage from Numbers to prophetic history in ancient Israel, especially to the Elohist tradition.

I. Contextualizing Biblical Prophecy

St. Paul transformed the subjunctive or qualitative mood of Moses' reply, "would that . . . ," into a clear, demonstrative sentence: "Whatever was written in former days was written for our instruction" (Rom. 15:4).[3] "Whatever was written" embraces not only the final moment of putting the words in writing but also the many stages of oral tradition from the original speaker to the leaders of prayer and instruction in the sacred assemblies of Israel. All contributed to the final form of the biblical text. This tradition of oral instruction and transmission lies behind such lines as:

Give ear, O heavens, and I will speak;
let the earth hear the words of my mouth.

2. Glen Lewandowski, O.S.C., "Would that all (God's people) were prophets," *Word and Event* 51 (1983, XIII.2): 10. (Available from the same address as in the source note above.)
3. Joseph A. Fitzmyer, "The Letter to the Romans," NJBC 51:49, comments upon a similar statement in Rom. 4:24, that Scripture was written "for our sake too: Paul has recalled the Abraham incident to apply it to his readers. He thus employs a feature of midrashic interpretation, the tendency to modernize or actualize the OT by applying it to a new situation" (R. Bloch, *DBSup* 3. 1263-65). Compare the later Midrash: "All that is recorded of Abraham is repeated in the history of his children" (Gen. Rabb. 40:8).

> May my teaching drop like the rain,
>> my speech condense like the dew.

> (Deut. 32:1-2)[4]

The oral transmission, interpretation, and application continues in the spirit of the Midrash into our own day.[5]

As we look back over the long tradition of speaking, repeating, writing, and speaking again what has been written, we need to avoid an easy mistake. We should not assume that the original moment, when Moses spoke the words of the Torah (so difficult to reconstruct), or the later moment when the passage received its final shape in the canonical book of Numbers are necessarily the only inspired moments nor necessarily the most inspired and important moments. The canonical moment provides a norm for all ages. Yet, the time of this definitive shaping of the Scriptures, generally placed in the post-exilic age, lacks the heroic, certainly the enthusiastic adrenalin of such periods of biblical life as the time of the prophetic bands[6] or of the classical prophets.[7] If the first or the last moment of the biblical text's transmission is not necessarily the holiest, certainly not necessarily the most appropriate, and if the text receives a new moment of strength and inspiration, like the Midrash, in our contemporary age, then we must respect the setting and contextualization, the challenge and the hope, of the world mission of biblical religion. The words of Moses receive an important nuance or specification as we adapt them: "Would that all the LORD's people in Japan or Korea, in Papua New Guinea or Indonesia, in the Sudan or Botswana were prophets!" Nor is it necessary to tell such people, whose lifestyle may correspond to that of Abraham, or Moses, or

4. Cf. Ps. 44:1: "We have heard with our ears, O God, our ancestors have told us, what deeds you performed in their days"; and Josh. 1:8, so important for the Qumran covenantors: "This book of the law shall not depart out of your mouth; you shall meditate on it day and night."

5. Cf. James A. Sanders, *From Sacred Story to Sacred Text* (Philadelphia: Fortress Press, 1987); Walter E. Rast, *Tradition and the Old Testament,* Guides to Biblical Scholarship (Philadelphia: Fortress Press, 1972); John Barton, *People of the Book?* (Louisville: Westminster/John Knox Press, 1988); Michael Fishbane, *Biblical Interpretation in Ancient Israel* (Oxford: Clarendon Press, 1985).

6. Cf. 1 Sam. 10:5-8.

7. Cf. Amos 3:8: "The lion has roared, who will not fear? The LORD God has spoken, who can but prophesy?" or Jer. 20:9, where God's word "is something like a burning fire shut up in my bones; I am weary with holding it in, and I cannot."

Samuel, that they must live a few more centuries or even millennia before they can rightly receive God's word of salvation.

Embedded in what we have just said is another, important rubric for interpreting Moses' words, "Would that all the LORD's people were prophets!" Everything that happened in the small area of Canaan or Israel over a wide expanse of time, almost two thousand years, is being relived now somewhere across the wide geographical expanse of planet earth in each small moment of our existence. Old Testament time was expansive (2,000 years) and its space minuscule (only 6,000 square miles of land); in the mission of biblical religion today time is minuscule (each moment), and space is as expansive as the earth. Somewhere today a family, tribe, or country is reliving the secular culture and religious response of each age and person in the Bible. Responding to the jealousy of modern Joshuas, people within the structure of church and synagogal authority, crying out against spontaneous prophetic speech, "My lord, stop them," Moses' words ring out: Let them prophesy, these new Eldads and Medads![8]

Since prophecy is at the heart of Numbers 11:29, a preliminary or descriptive definition of prophecy is appropriate. Relying upon the investigations of David L. Petersen,[9] we conclude that prophecy was not an office in Israel like priest or elder but a quality of someone who occupied any one of these offices or other responsibilities in Israel. Prophecy was a unique calling from God, to speak out or to act forcefully in the name of the ancient covenant (particularly with northern prophets) or in the name of decency and honesty (with southern prophets); a fearlessness in standing up against any human authority, even though it be divinely validated as priest or king, and not only correcting it but also declaring its demise, should it not reform.

With these qualities in mind, we conclude to this definition: prophets are those persons (1) so fully and consistently members of their community and in touch with its charism and rounding inspiration, (2) so perceptive of events and people in their world and articulate in getting the attention

---

8. We recall one of the final statements of Karl Rahner about Vatican II, the ecumenical council of the Roman Catholic Church. He declared that with the council the church is at the threshold of becoming a world church. From its new mission to the world it must learn the implications of its prophetic sentences in the council documents. Cf. "Towards a Fundamental Theological Interpretation of Vatican II," *Theological Studies* 40 (December 1979): 716-27.

9. David L. Petersen, *The Roles of Israel's Prophets,* JSOTSup 17 (Sheffield: JSOT, 1981).

of their contemporaries that (3) as a result they bring the internal challenge of the community's conscience — its hopes and ideals — to bear upon the external form of the community's lifestyle and work.[10] Prophecy, therefore, was always challenging any unjust, proud, or greedy expression of religion by reaching back to religion's ancient, inspired ideals, thereby enabling religion to be back on track as it reached toward the future.

In this sense prophecy itself was subject to correction and reform, as we find to be the result of the passage of Numbers 11:29. In the following chapter of Numbers, Moses is supreme above all prophets. Deuteronomy 34:10 concludes the Torah or basic law books of Israel by declaring: "Never since has there arisen a prophet in Israel like Moses." Prophecy, perhaps more so than any other form of leadership in ancient Israel or in the early church, evolved in its various roles. This statement is put very simply in 1 Samuel 9:9, "Formerly in Israel, anyone who went to inquire of God would say, 'Come, let us go to the seer *(ro'eh)*'; for the one who is now called a prophet *(nabi')* was formerly called a seer."

While prophecy, therefore, is deeply rooted in tradition, it is always addressing the contemporary moment. The present cultural and religious setting, in fact, adds a necessary ingredient to the prophetic message before we arrive at what God is saying to us in the biblical, prophetic word. Prophecy does not bring the letter but the heroic spirit of the past into each new moment of time and into each new place of ministry. World geography and its diverse cultures contribute to prophetic interpretation.

In our contemporary one-world, we cannot become truly prophetic until our prophecy becomes universal. How appropriate, then, the qualifying adjective *all* in the statement at the center of this study, "Would that all the LORD's people were prophets!" Prophecy itself is best understood as a qualifying adjective, distinguishing the exercise of traditional offices or a person's normal work and duties. Yet, this secondary role so transformed the accepted values and beliefs of Israel's religion that this "religion [evolved] into something scarcely paralleled in the ancient world."[11] The office of elders, which Numbers 11 ascribes to a special intervention of Moses, is shown by Exodus 18 to have originated in the suggestion of Moses' father-in-law, the Midianite priest Jethro. What was first inspired outside of Israel is transformed within Israel by its prophetic charism.

10. Cf. Carroll Stuhlmueller, "Prophet, Who are You?" *The Biblical Heritage,* Bruce Walter Festschrift (Welmington Del.: Michael Glazier, 1986): 75, 82.
11. John Barton, *Oracles of God* (Oxford: Oxford University Press, 1988): 272.

We now proceed to investigate Numbers 11:29 in its complex but exceptionally rich setting in the Bible. We will study an important implication of Numbers 11:29, namely, that Israelite religion and prophecy developed from the secular area of life, often enough from its peripheral or insignificant events. Even Moses' incidental response in Numbers 11:29, defending Eldad and Medad against Joshua's misplaced fervor and blatant jealousy, may have originated in exasperation, yet it later becomes a key sentence in the theological development of Israelite prophecy.

II. Numbers 11:29 within the Elohist Tradition

Robert R. Wilson wrote that chapter 11 of Numbers manifests a "complex literary and tradition history,"[12] and J. de Vaulx speaks about "the juxtaposition of diverse elements [and] a redaction most complex."[13] In a recent commentary Rita J. Burns writes more specifically:

> The wilderness stories in Numbers were recorded by Yahwist and/or Elohist sources and in many cases these early traditions were later supplemented and reshaped by the Priestly writer.[14]

We attempt to unravel some of this complexity by concentrating on one of the four sources of the Pentateuch, that of the Elohist. We will notice at first a positive approach toward prophecy and then a growing distrust toward it and its decentralizing form of religious life. This negative attitude shows up in the Priestly writer who shaped the Pentateuch. By wrestling with this complex literary and historical situation we will discover many ways by which Numbers 11–12 intercepts world ministry today.

An outline of Numbers 11–12 will clarify some of the crisscrossing of traditions:[15]

12. Robert R. Wilson, *Prophecy and Society in Ancient Israel* (Philadelphia: Fortress Press, 1980): 151.

13. J. de Vaulx, *Les Nombres,* Sources Bibliques (Paris: Gabalda, 1972): 148, 149.

14. Rita J. Burns, *Exodus, Leviticus, Numbers,* OTM, 3 (Wilmington, Del.: Michael Glazier, 1983): 220.

15. Cf. Wilson, op. cit., 151-53.

11:1-3   The people complain against Moses and are saved by his intercession.

11:4-9   A negative story about the people's greed, despite the gift of manna.

11:10-17   A positive story about Moses' burden in caring for the people and the Lord's answer in the choice of elders.

11:18-23   A continuation of the negative story.

11:24-30   Again the positive story, with the Lord's validation of the elders by granting them the prophetic spirit.

11:31-34   Once more the negative story, with the Lord's answer to the greedy people by punishing them through the food they devoured.

12:1-16   Miriam and Aaron complain against Moses; Moses intercedes for Miriam.

The editor wove these various strands together splendidly: the intercession of Moses within the first and last episodes; in between, the interchange of negative and positive stories as well as the cycle of burdens and God's answer. The people's and Moses' burden over their troubles is met by God through the assistance of elders for Moses and the gift of quail for the people's hunger. Moreover, the episodes of elders and quail are knit together by the Hebrew word *ruah,* which can be translated either "spirit" or "wind."[16] As spirit, the *ruah* rests upon each of the elders that they may share in the office of Moses; as wind, the *ruah* brings the quail. We will return to this crisscross of traditions and interweaving of stories. First, we attend more closely to the positive story of the elders in Numbers 11:16-17, 24-30.

In Numbers 11 God directs Moses to institute the office of elder. Moses is told to "gather for me seventy of the elders of Israel, whom you know to be the elders of the people and officers over them. . . . I will take some of the spirit that is on you and put it on them, and they shall bear the burden of the people along with you . . ." (Num. 11:16-17). Elders, accordingly, are to be notable for their trustworthiness, wisdom, and popular acceptance. They are people loyal to Moses and the ancient traditions of Israel. Not born into the office like the Levites and priests and, later, the kings, they represent a strong momentum toward decentralization and the sharing of authority, typical of the Mosaic age.

16. Cf. de Vaulx, op. cit., 155.

The Hebrew text highlights the exceptionally important, even mysterious entitlement of the elders. As Sawyer remarks: "The term translated 'take' (vv. 17, 25) . . . occurs only here and looks like an isolated relic of ancient semitechnical language. [This] unique expression heightens the numinous effect of the description."[17] Another, this time common Hebrew word for prophesying in verse 27, (NRSV: "are prophesying") appears in the intensive, reflective form of the verb.[18] The NEB translates it, "They fell into a prophetic ecstasy." The effects of this form of prophecy stirred spontaneous reactions. Prophecy was so contagious that Eldad and Medad began prophesying. It incited an immediate reaction among the people. A young man quickly ran to Joshua, whose response was jealousy and anger. The phenomenon was so striking that the Bible never tells us what they said. Or did prophecy consist in unusual, dramatic behavior? Prophecy expected a total involvement of the person.[19]

Prophecy, therefore, does not create the office of elders but authenticates it in the eyes of all the people.[20] These men were not ordained to be prophets but to be elders; in the midst of performing their office as elders, moments of prophetic insight and contagious enthusiasm broke forth.

The next incident insists upon the free gift of prophecy. Prophecy is not a prerogative of any institution, nor is it bestowed only in a sacred place like a meeting tent or shrine, nor again in the immediate presence of a holy person like Moses:

> Two men remained in the camp, one named Eldad, and the other named Medad, and the spirit rested on them; they were among those registered, but they had not gone out to the [sacred meeting] tent, and so they prophesied in the camp. (Num. 11:26)

At this point the famous incident, the theme of this study, occurred.

> A young man ran and told Moses, "Eldad and Medad are prophesying in the camp." And Joshua son of Nun, the assistant of Moses, one of his

---

17. Cf. Sawyer, op. cit., 8.

18. This verb never occurs in the simple (qal) form, only in the passive or intensive (niphal or hithpael); the noun derived from it, *nabi'*, is one of the most common words for prophet, with a sequence of vowels, a-i, frequent in words that denote passivity (cf. R. Rendtorff, *TDNT,* VI:796).

19. Cf. Wilson, op. cit., 154.

20. Cf. Wilson, op. cit., 153.

chosen men, said, "My lord Moses, stop them." But Moses said to him: "Are you jealous for my sake? Would that all the LORD's people were prophets, and that the LORD would put [the divine] spirit on them!" (Num. 11:27-29)

This entire account firmly establishes and honors the institution of elders by its association with Moses. It expects, at least, occasional manifestations of prophetic fervor, even if the normal qualities for an elder are honesty, wisdom, and acceptability. In Israel authority is to be shared, not restricted. It can blossom suddenly in places least expected, in the secular arena of daily living, in the "camp." Moreover, as Conrad E. l'Heureux remarks: "The acknowledgement of Eldad and Medad's prophetic charism by Moses against the objections of Joshua, serves to protect the independence of the prophetic office [perhaps a better phrase would be "prophetic *role*"] from those who would subject it to institutional control."[21] Because of a similarity of words and context with 1 Samuel 10, some commentators see here "an attempt to legitimate Israel's adaptation of the Canaanite phenomenon of ecstatic prophecy."[22] This acceptance of non-Israelite forms of religious expression will be seen more clearly as we relate Numbers 11 to other parts of the Pentateuch.

Numbers 11–12 is linked to other sections of the Pentateuch by belonging, according to many scholars, to the Elohist or "E" tradition. The Elohist fragments, as Wolff refers to them,[23] are admittedly difficult to detect and are even denied by some scholars like Paul Volz, Wilhelm Rudolph, and Sigmund Mowinckel.[24] The Elohist material, originating in the north, survived in fragmentary ways within other material that was rooted in a southern, Jerusalem base. These southern Priestly editors tended to be suspicious of prophetic developments. We look at several of these prophetic fragments within the Elohist fragments, at times abruptly introduced.

Genesis 20 gives the Elohist account of the patriarch's presenting his wife as only his sister![25] The foreign king Abimelech of Gerar shows up

21. Conrad E. l'Heureux, "Numbers," *NJBC,* 5:27.

22. Burns, op. cit., 229.

23. H. W. Wolff, "The Elohistic Fragments in the Pentateuch," *The Vitality of Old Testament Traditions,* 2nd & 3rd ed. (Atlanta: John Knox Press, 1982): 67.

24. Cf., Alan W. Jenks, *The Elohist and North Israelite Traditions* (Chico, Calif.: Scholars Press, 1977): 1; T. E. Fretheim, "Elohist," *IDBSup,* 259-63.

25. The Yahwist account occurs in Gen. 12:10-20.

as a God-fearing man, seriously intent on doing what is right. Honesty becomes an important aspect of leadership. When Abraham intercedes for Abimelech, the latter's wife and maidservants again bear children. Abraham is here called a "prophet," in Hebrew a *nabi'*.[26] We are reminded of Moses' intercession for the people and for his sister Miriam and brother Aaron in Numbers 11–12.

The crucial role of the foreigner becomes still more apparent in another Elohist story, that in Exodus 18. Here the office of elder is traced to Moses' father-in-law, Jethro, a Midianite priest. Like Abimelech, he, too, is called "a man who fears God." And as Wolff writes, "What follows shows that here 'fear of God' means being reliable and rejecting dishonest gain."[27] The foreign origin of prophecy shows up again in the Elohist tradition with the sudden appearance of "Balaam, son of Beor [who lived] at Pethor which is on the Euphrates in the land of Amaw" (Num. 22:5). Balaam's moment of greatness is linked with integrity,[28] his eventual execution as a criminal with venality and sensuality.[29] The Elohist maintained severe moral requirements for prophecy.

Already the Bible is flashing some warning signal about prophecy. True, the entire institution at times manifested heroic greatness in defending the poor and in loyally returning to the roots of the Mosaic revelation. This we see in the story of Elijah (1 Kings 17–21), closely related to the Elohist tradition in the Pentateuch.[30] Yet, the very next chapter in 1 Kings tells of "prophet against prophet," the title of Simon John DeVries' monograph.[31] So decadent did prophecy become that the first of a new type of prophets, Amos from Tekoa, flatly declared: "I am no prophet, not a member of any prophetic guild."[32] A later prophet, Micah, condemns the members of the prophetic guilds for their greed and manipulative practices:

26. Cf. Jenks, op. cit., 21.

27. Wolff, op. cit., 74.

28. Cf. Num. 22:18.

29. Cf. Num. 25; 31:8, 16.

30. Cf. Jenks, op. cit., 100-101.

31. Simon John DeVries, *Prophet Against Prophet* (Grand Rapids: Eerdmans, 1978).

32. Amos 7:14, my translation. Cf. H. W. Wolff, *Joel and Amos,* Hermeneia (Philadelphia: Fortress Press, 1977): 312-13. While Shalom M. Paul, *Amos,* Hermeneia (Minneapolis: Fortress Press, 1991): 238, 246-47, favors a translation in the past tense, "I was not a prophet nor was I a member of a prophetic guild," he admits the ambiguity of the Hebrew text, the possibility of a "present tense," and stresses the divine intervention for Amos's prophetic career.

Thus says the LORD concerning the prophets
> who lead my people astray,
who cry "Peace"
> when they have something to eat,
but sanctify[33] a war against those
> who put nothing into their mouths.

> (Mic. 3:5)

In other words, feed their bellies properly and these prophets will say whatever their wealthy donor wants! The priest Amaziah implied that Amos prophesied for pay, saying to him: "O seer, go, flee away to the land of Judah, earn your bread there, and prophesy there" (Amos 7:12).[34]

Returning to the Elohist passage in Numbers 11, we draw some conclusions from this history of prophecy's decline. We understand why the priesthood at Jerusalem, in editing the material, introduced subtle shifts toward a more cautious view of prophecy. This editor surrounded the account of elder-prophets with the negative account of the people's clamoring for more tasty food than "this manna" (Num. 11:6). This passage almost seems like a condemnation of the venal prophets in Micah's time. Prophets, moreover, had to be reminded not to pretend to be another Moses. In fact, they stand corrected and judged by this supremely holy chosen one:

When there are prophets among you,
> I the LORD make myself known to them in visions,
> I speak to them in dreams.
Not so with my servant Moses;
> he is entrusted with all my house.
With him I speak face to face — clearly, not in riddles;
> and he beholds the form of the LORD.

> (Num. 12:6-8)[35]

33. The Hebrew uses the word *qadesh* to separate and so sanctify for God.
34. Cf. 1 Sam. 9:5-8, where Saul and his servant are worried lest they do not have a proper stipend for the "man of God" or "seer."
35. The tension does not seem to have arisen from the fact of Moses' Cushite wife, as mentioned at the beginning of chapter 12, but, rather, as Robert R. Wilson wrote, "with a dispute over prophetic authority" (op. cit., 155). Elsewhere Miriam is said to have been a prophetess (Exod. 15:20).

The Elohist tradition in Numbers 11 is also seen to veer away from the freer, more secular expression of authority in Exodus 18. In Numbers 11 Jethro's name has been washed out; it is the Lord who commands Moses to ordain elders. This investiture takes place before the sacred tent of meeting. Another restriction of the prophetic element appears in the Hebrew text of Numbers 11:25, translated literally by the NRSV: "But they did not do so again," that is, prophesy. By a slight change of vowels, the verb can be traced to the root *'asap,* different from *sup,* found in our present Hebrew Bible, as was done long ago by the Samaritan Pentateuch; or it can be traced to still another root, as we see in Aramaic versions of the Targum, especially of Jonathan, and in the Latin Vulgate.[36] As a result the phrase reads: "They did not cease from prophesying." The New American Bible makes still another emendation to arrive at a positive interpretation.[37] This intricate textual work leads to some serious doubts about the negative tone of our Hebrew text; a more positive reading may have been original.[38] Later, when prophecy fell into disfavor with religious authorities at Jerusalem and also with the classical prophets, the negative overtones were emphasized. The text thus modulated to its present form, disassociating the elders from prophecy.

Still other restrictions and complications caught up with Numbers 11. The openness to foreign influences and the non-complimentary correction of Joshua bothered later Jewish commentators. The Aramaic Targums, recited in the synagogue, explained that Joshua wanted Eldad and Medad silenced for reasons of personal modesty; they were announcing his succession to the role of Moses.[39] Moses, therefore, according to this interpretation, was not speaking in defense of the free gift of the spirit for everyone to prophesy but, rather, was defending the institutional line of authority and the naming of his successor!

The interpretation of Exodus 18 and Numbers 11 continued to evolve. Christian writers recognized in these passages a defense of gentile sources of

36. Cf. de Vaulx, op. cit., 156-57.
37. Cf. *Textual Notes on Old Testament Readings* (Washington, D.C.: Catholic Biblical Association, 1970), which joins the final words of v. 25 to v. 26 and changes these last two Hebrew words (NRSV: "But they did not do so again") to "were not in the gathering" so that the resulting translation is: ". . . they prophesied [v. 26]. Now two men, one named Eldad and the other Medad, *were not in the gathering* but had been left in the camp."
38. For further discussion, see Martin Noth, *Numbers,* OTL (Philadelphia: Westminster, 1968): 89; Burns, op. cit., 228.
39. Cf. de Vaulx, op. cit., 156-57.

inspiration, at times even with anti-Jewish innuendo. Origen and Clement perceived in Exodus 18 Moses' willingness to learn "divine truths from a pagan priest, . . . a warrant for seeking knowledge from non-Christians." Cyril of Alexandria viewed Jethro as a foreshadowing of the Christian faith in being converted from an older, inferior faith to the new, superior faith.[40] Cyril was following an earlier Jewish tradition that Jethro converted to the faith of Moses.

With quiet understatement de Vaulx writes: "No one is surprised that a text so complex and also so nuanced as this one, the fruit of a long elaboration, has been interpreted diversely."[41] To apply this long, intricate tradition about prophecy and the office of elders to our own contemporary world of ministry, we attach these reflections.

Significant religious movements emerge from non-biblical, non-Christian sources. Also from our own Christian ranks, insignificant people like Eldad and Medad, never again heard of in the Bible, continue to be summoned freely by God for religious offices in the church and synagogue. Sadly enough, the original Elohist source warns us, we can show ourselves as jealous and outraged as Joshua: "My lord Moses, stop them!" Happily enough, God will find a way to respond:

"Are you jealous for my sake? Would that all the LORD's people were prophets, and that the LORD would put [the divine] spirit on them!"

The Pentateuch accepts Israel's dependence upon world resources and non-Mosaic expressions of worship. Are we able, with biblical humility and openness, to recognize and receive the rich developments of culture and styles of leadership across our world? Are we close enough to this outside world[42] to appreciate what other world religions offer us?

Jethro's advice and the emergence of Eldad and Medad from the secular camp seemed to happen almost by chance. In Exodus 18 Jethro finds Moses on this particular occasion, not wrapt in contemplation on top of Mount Sinai,[43] nor alone with the Lord in the sacred tent of meeting,[44]

40. Cf. Brevard S. Childs, *The Book of Exodus,* OTL (Philadelphia: Westminster Press, 1974): 333.
41. de Vaulx, op. cit., 156.
42. Moses married into a Midianite or Cushite family. His father-in-law was a "pagan" priest: cf. Exod. 2:15-22; 18:1; Num. 12:1.
43. Cf. Exod. 24:18; 34:28.
44. Cf. Exod. 34:34.

nor silent and supremely humble,[45] but over-involved in secular business. In Numbers 11 we are never told why Eldad and Medad remained behind in the camp while an important ceremony was taking place at the tent of meeting. Are we quiet enough to hear the voice of prophecy from unlikely, even accidental situations? Or does the solemn sound of chant and meticulous movement of ritual mute the happenings of the world of Eldad and Medad? Do we restrict the gifts of the spirit to sacred places of worship or to people ordained or invested with religious authority?

Charismatic prophecy declined and needed to be corrected both by new forms of prophecy and by the more stable forms of leadership at Jerusalem.[46] Prophecy is not for its own sake, nor does its certification by God bestow on it an unconditional charter of holiness and truth. Prophecy and institutional offices today will survive within church and synagogue only by enrichment and correction, mutually from one another, but principally from outside themselves.

Moses' exclamation, "Would that all the LORD's people were prophets!" as diversely interpreted within biblical tradition, places before us a challenge, a hope, and a warning. Pastorally we must decide which of these moments of biblical history applies to our particular situation. As mentioned already, the latest period of biblical history is no holier than the first. Each has been written for our instruction.[47]

Conclusions

After each section of this study we have reflected upon the impact today of Numbers 11:29 and its larger setting within the Bible and within biblical tradition. We conclude with a few, general observations.

---

45. Cf. Num. 12:3.

46. Cf. Wilson, op. cit., 154.

47. We are reminded of the crisp sentence of James A. Sanders, "the false prophets invoked an otherwise decently good theology but at the wrong time, supporting leaders and people when they needed a challenge" ("Hermeneutics in True and False Prophecy," op. cit., 96). Earlier on pp. 92-93, Sanders cites the example of the prophet Hananiah in Jeremiah 28, "a person who had real knowledge but was a prisoner of that knowledge. Parroting Isaiah, he was satisfied to repeat a solution of the past; for with all his knowledge of history he did not know how to listen [to] history 'becoming.' He knew only the eternal return of the wheel, but not the scales of history which tremble like a human heart."

Each major biblical passage, like Moses' exclamation, "Would that all the LORD's people were prophets!" needs interpretation against the environment where we minister God's word. The Bible itself did not slavishly apply the earlier inspired word but adapted it, positively or negatively, according to new, local conditions.

Prophecy, like biblical religion today, proceeds on its pilgrim way and is being summoned "to that continual reformation of which she always has need, insofar as she is an institution of men [and women] here on earth."[48]

The canonical shape of the Bible points out the need of church unity, where institutions are preserved by elders and by other religious leaders and are challenged by prophets. Here, too, insignificant secular events are turned from occasional responses into enduring tradition. Because of Jerusalem we hear the echoing challenge of Moses, "Would that all the LORD's people were prophets!"

The Bible sanctions the initiative to seek the insignificant events in each one's culture and locale, those small episodes, those sleeping talents and ideals in youth, those age-old seasoned instructions from our "Jethros," be these people, again like Jethro, even pagan priests. All can be turned into the eternal word of God. Among the insignificant moments are those that happen suddenly. "Keep awake therefore, for you know neither the day nor the hour" (Matt. 23:13).

48. The language is certainly of Protestant vintage, whose influence, however, appears in an official document of the Roman Catholic Church. This quotation is from Vatican II's constitution on Ecumenism, *Unitatis Redintegratio,* chap. II, n. 6, *Vatican Council II,* ed. Austin Flannery, O.P. (Collegeville, Minn.: Liturgical Press, 1975): 459.

The Ashes of the Red Heifer: Religious Ceremonies and Obedience to Torah

JEROME R. MALINO

"It is we who sanctify life. Purity and impurity do not inhere in objects, rites, or ceremonies."

The passage under consideration has been an embarrassment to some, a puzzlement to many, and a curiosity to all its readers. It is part of the annual cycle of synagogue Scripture readings and is read in traditional synagogues three weeks before the Passover to remind the community of the importance of approaching that festival in a state of ritual purity.

This text is an isolated one, having no connection with what appears before it or with what follows it. It tells of the ingredients and the effects of the purifying water to be used in the case of the pollution that derives from contact with a dead body.

In Leviticus 5 we read of the uncleanness that derives from contact with the carcass of a beast, cattle, or an insect and the offerings required to remove that uncleanness are listed. In Leviticus 22 we learn of the pollution of a priest from similar contact, and the Nazirite, during the period of his vow, may not be in the presence of a corpse, even that of his own family. While contamination by contact with a corpse is, as we have seen, noted in other places, it is only here that a mode of purification is prescribed.

144

It is also to be noted that here the uncleanness reaches everyone who comes into the tent of a person who has died, it touches every open vessel, and it derives from contact with a body in an open field.

The mode of purification that is here described makes possible a return to a state of "kedusha" or sanctification. It is needed for both vessels and people. Most specially to be noted are the words in verse 9, *chatat hi,* appearing in our translation as, "it is for cleansing"; in the Revised English Bible it is "a purification offering." The old Jewish Publication Society translation of 1917 reads, "it is a purification from sin." Those words will help us to understand the way in which an ancient folk custom was introduced into the sacred ritual of the priesthood.

The notion that a dead body pollutes is both primitive and widespread; evidence of it is found on the American, the African, and the Asian continents and appears in the cultures of ancient Greece and Rome. It has been described as a popular custom, only later made a part of priestly statutes. It was this association with priestly regulations that kept the custom of the ashes of the red heifer alive but also separated it from its original meaning.

The basis for so elaborate a practice lies in the belief that contact with a corpse produced the most severe impurity and it was not to be cleansed by ordinary water or any simple process. It was believed that the spirit of the dead could exert control over anyone who had contact with the body. What was required was a ceremonial process of exorcism. The ashes and the red color (like blood!) are known from folklore to be a means of protection from evil spirits. So strong was the hold of ancient custom on the thought and behavior of the people that even though it reflected idolatrous antecedents, it could not be discontinued and had, instead, to be incorporated into priestly procedures.

According to Jacob Milgrom, in the Jewish Publication Society commentary to the book of Numbers,[1] corpse contamination "evoked an obsessive irrational fear in individuals." This helps us to understand the persistence of some purifying practice through various stages of religious development. In the biblical tradition this purifying practice became the *chatat,* generally translated as a "purification offering." Since it is the blood that does the contaminating, the blood of the red cow was poured on the horns of the altar, a homeopathic process by which the source of the contamination is also the means for its removal. Here we must note

---

1. *Numbers,* The Torah Commentary (New York: Jewish Publication Society, 5750/1990): 441.

the seeming paradox in which the same substance that provides purification for the contamination also contaminates those who are in contact with it. In the purifying process the ashes of the red heifer absorb the impurity they are meant to remove and become impure in the process.

The significance of incorporating an ancient and popular ceremony of exorcism into the sacrificial system must not be overlooked. It represents a transition from magic to religion. Whatever may have been the original intent in the use of the ashes of the red heifer for purification purposes, once introduced into the sacrificial system, the steps taken were no longer due to the inherent power of the objects being used to change the unclean into the clean but became, instead, part of a larger ceremonial system in which the efficacy of the ceremonies performed derived from obedience to God's law, not from the specific, and magical, properties of the agents used. This transition from magic to religion is reflected in a tale told in the Midrash to the book of Numbers, about Rabbi Johanan ben Zakkai in an exchange with his students.

> An idolater asked R. Johanan b. Zakkai: "These rites that you perform look like a kind of witchcraft. You bring a heifer, burn it, pound it, and take its ashes. If one of you is defiled by a dead body you sprinkle upon him two or three drops and say to him: 'Thou art clean!' " R. Johanan asked him: "Has the demon of madness ever possessed you?" "No," he replied. "Have you ever seen a man possessed by this demon of madness?" "Yes," said he. "And what do you do in such a case?" "We bring roots," he replied, "and make them smoke under him, then we sprinkle water upon the demon and it flees." Said R. Johanan to him: "Let your ears hear what you utter with your mouth! Precisely so is this spirit a spirit of uncleanness. Water of purification is sprinkled upon the unclean and the spirit flees." When the idolater had gone R. Johanan's disciples said to their master: "Master! This man you have put off with a mere makeshift but what explanation will you give to us?" Said he to them: "By your life! It is not the dead that defiles nor the water that purifies! The Holy One, blessed be He, merely says: 'I have laid down a statute, I have issued a decree. You are not allowed to transgress My decree.' "

Rabbi Johanan does not try to give to his students the rationale for the practice, which was satisfactory for the inquiring pagan. The questioner came from a different religious culture, one that made it readily comprehensible to him that the impurity of contamination with a corpse could be drawn out of a person through contact with the ashes of the red heifer and water. For the pagan the test lay in the magical efficacy of the cleansing object. The example, given by Rabbi Johanan, addressed precisely that point. For his Jewish students that "efficacy" had no pertinence whatsoever. The contaminated object was cleansed simply because the divine text said it was, not because of anything that had happened to it per se.

The account of the red heifer is one of four Torah laws that cannot be explained by human reason but that, nevertheless, demands obedience. The remaining three laws are: the requirement of a man to marry the widow of his childless brother (Deut. 25:5-10); the injunction against wearing garments woven of different threads (Deut. 22:11); the sending of the goat into the wilderness, to Azazel (Lev. 16). It is said that even Solomon, who learned the logic of all of God's commandments, was unable to discern the logic of the red heifer. In the absence of any compelling logical reasoning, it is not surprising that our passage under discussion evoked a variety of poetic, metaphoric, and homiletical responses.

The dictionary definition of magic is, "the art which is believed to produce effects by a mastery of secret forces in nature." By contrast, religion does not seek to control the forces of nature (except for those religions that still retain some of the elements of magic) but seeks to effect the spirit and life of the individual. Even when a rite or ceremony, once practiced for its "magical mastery of secret forces in nature," is continued as part of religious practice it serves an altogether different purpose. Its "efficacy" derives not from its magic but from the psychological and spiritual qualities brought to the practice by the religious person who is able to make the heritage of the past serve the spiritual needs of the present.

It is in this way that the Torah incorporated folk fear and folk custom into its sophisticated sacrificial system, making possible such spiritual approach as that of Rabbi Samson Raphael Hirsch, a rabbi in Germany in the nineteenth century. Rabbi Hirsch saw the ceremony of the red heifer as a reflection of the tension between body and soul. Every corpse proclaims the mortality of all humanity and calls attention to the finiteness of human existence and human inability to effect any change in this regard. By contrast, the expiating *chatat* purges the sinner and directs all of us "to the sphere of morals," an area in which we are not helpless creatures dealing with our fragile mortality but individuals who can exercise a freedom of choice between what is pure and impure. The "metaphor" of the red heifer suggests to us a way of looking at all aspects of life and tells us that we can ransom the unclean for the sake of the pure. Our physical lack of freedom threatens us and frightens us in our helplessness. The laws of purity remind us that in matters of morality, we are in control. "Human beings can be free of sin, can become so and remain so."

The medieval Hebrew commentator Rashi, in the name of Rabbi Moshe the Preacher, says that the heifer came to atone for the calf. "The sin of the golden calf was from a lack of faith and, as appropriate penitence, the commandment of the heifer was given to them. It was a statute, a commandment with no logic, and its observance could come only from the strength of faith." Not even the trespass of the golden calf was immune to the benign ministration of the red heifer's atonement.

The modern religious person understands that the faith by which he or she lives transcends reason not through the compelling force of a written text, no matter how venerable, but by the compelling sense of ethical and moral responsibility. Those commandments of the Lord, by which we feel constrained to live, derive their authority not only from tradition but from the conviction that they are written large in the fabric of reality and are as ineluctable as the laws that govern the physical universe. They command our unquestioning allegiance and do not allow the tempering and tampering of specious logic.

It is we who sanctify life. Purity and impurity do not inhere in objects, rites, or ceremonies. It is we who ascribe sanctity to things. It is we who can put all things to noble purpose. It is we who can rise above our frail mortality and make the profane holy and the impure pure. The prophet said, "The righteous will live by his Faith." As we seek to put all things base to noble purpose and search for the sacred even in the profane, though we be of mortal flesh, yet do we hold eternity in our hearts.

Hear, O Israel: Law and Love in Deuteronomy

BLU GREENBERG

*"For a Jew to say, 'I will' or 'I do' is as powerful
a statement of love as it is to say the words
'I love' or 'I believe.'"*

The Covenant

Moses is about to die, after serving his people for forty years. Joshua is to take up the reins. The people are finally at the threshold of entering the promised land. It is time for a farewell speech. The book of Deuteronomy!

Deuteronomy, or *devarim* ("words") in Hebrew, is not one but three farewell addresses by Moses. As any good leader should, Moses reviews the history of the people under his leadership, refers to his accomplishments, and introduces his successor. More important, he wishes to ensure a continuity of belief and shared values, in particular faithfulness to the source of power and authority, YHWH.

Yet, Deuteronomy is much more than a last will and testament of Moses or a ceremony of succession for Joshua. It is, essentially and throughout, a Book of the Covenant; not merely a recapitulation of Sinai but another complete act of covenanting the people to God.

What is the overall function of the covenant in the grand design of human life grounded in God? Judaism is a religion of redemption that promises the physical and spiritual perfection of the world. The earth will be made into a paradise, and the fullness of knowledge and of love between God and humanity will be achieved. The vehicle for this achievement is the covenant, a special partnership motivated by love between God and humanity, in which the pacesetter and teacher is God's chosen people. The most extended and nuanced statement of the centrality of the covenant in Judaism is found in the book of Deuteronomy. Its distinctive thrust is particularly expressed in two ways: (1) it is a covenant of love and of law, not of political fidelities; (2) the sacred covenant between human beings and God incorporates within itself civil laws and societal ethics. Thus, the law of the stranger (Deut. 10:19-20) or the law of weights and measures (Deut. 25:13-16) is intimately connected to the belief in one God; in fact, observing these laws becomes a measure, a corollary, a tangible expression of belief in one God.

A Covenant of Love

Deuteronomy is a magnificent work, rich with multiple themes: struggle against idolatry, centralization of worship and containment of sacrifice, loyalty to one God, divine election and chosenness, faithfulness to the covenant, observance of the law, and inheritance of the land. Or, to reduce it to a simple equation: the children of Israel must be faithful to YHWH alone and follow the divine laws; YHWH in return will give them the land of Israel and a life of blessing and of continued life.

What is the nature of the covenant relationship? It is based on a mutual love. The covenant is the fruit of love, the expression of love and not its replacement or alternative.

> . . . For you are a holy people unto YHWH your God [who has] chosen you to be a special nation from among all the nations of the earth. Not because of your numbers did God desire you and choose you from among all the nations — for you are the smallest of them — but because God loved you and because he would keep the oath He swore to your ancestors. . . . (Deut. 7:6-8)

True, there is an element of arbitrariness — chosenness — in this covenant of love. The text teaches that chosenness, because of the love, is for purposes of a special holiness or purity or responsibility, not for a particular superiority (Deut. 7:1-5, 7-8; 9:4-5). The love, like all love, is unique to this special person or group. But it does not foreclose God's love for others as well.

This special bond is eternal. Each generation accepts it for itself. Yet, each also accepts it for those that follow.

> It is not with you alone that I make this covenant and oath, but with him who stands here with us this day and . . . also with him who is not here with us this day. (Deut. 29:4)

The covenant is not to be rescinded or replaced or forfeited. It never becomes an old testament but an ongoing one. Even when the people sin, the covenant is not over. Not sacrifice but repentance and confession will restore the relationship (Deut. 30:1-6).

Thus the covenant grows out of a love so powerful that it ultimately, and time and again, overrides all conditions and failures; it proves to be unconditional and unforfeitable. And because each partner turns to the other even when all appears to be lost, the covenant proves to be irrevocable and everlasting. Because the covenant was in their bones, not just in their minds, because of an inherent — or perhaps inherited — ability to stand inside of this love relationship, the Jewish partners throughout the generations were able to hear the admonitions and threats and even the curses in a different way. They heard these texts not merely as texts of terror, nor as descriptions of an exclusively stern and wrathful God (as some have described the God of Deuteronomy), but as the voice of a momentarily disappointed lover or distressed parent, sometimes stern but always loving.

> And you shall consider it in your heart that, as a man chastens his son, so YHWH your God chastens you. (Deut. 8:5)

It is no wonder that more than any other book of the Bible, the verses and phrases of Deuteronomy found their way into Jewish liturgical life. In addition to the *Shma Yisrael* (Deut. 6:4-9), some of "these words" are spoken at every peak moment of prayer, individual and communal.

Covenant, Law, and Love

The most remarkable aspect of this covenant, however, is its connection to the law. Acceptance of the covenant is no mere declaration of infatuation or allegiance. It embodies a most serious commitment, that of wholehearted observance of the law. Two things are unusual about this connection of law and covenant: One is that the law was subsumed under the covenant altogether. This is in sharp contrast to other ancient covenants of suzerainty treaties that were almost exclusively declarations of fealty or testaments of political allegiance. The second is the continuous coupling of love and law.

In Deuteronomy we find both sacred and secular law, at times existing side by side, sometimes in the same unit of laws (Deut. 16:8-13). Surprising as it is to find civil law in a covenant of faith, more unusual is it that no distinctions were made. The discovery about style confirmed that which is known to every Jewish child almost from the moment of understanding: that both are and carry the weight of God's law. The line between sacred and secular is overcome. Life is holistically holy.

The Ten Commandments embody this equation of different kinds of law. In addition to the concept of two tablets (Deut. 4:13; 10:4), which later tradition divided into five commandments each (by sheer volume the division would be quite different), the content itself suggests two distinct sections. The first five injunctions — monotheism, prohibition against idolatry, prohibition against using God's name for false oaths, the Sabbath, and honoring one's parents — all reflect the divine sphere. They all contain the phrase "YHWH your God." The laws of the second section reflect the ethical and moral fabric of society. Thou shalt not murder, commit adultery, steal, bear false witness, covet they neighbor's wife and possessions. These laws are delivered in terse tones; no reward or reason is given for they are unnecessary. They are laws that are guided by the principles of human reciprocity; without adherence to them society could not survive.

Some have asked, what is unique about the Decalogue? All of the commandments appear elsewhere in the Pentateuch, many more than once. Many answers have been put forth, including that they all are given in the second person singular, are independent of life on a national land, are given as categorical imperatives with no details spelled out (i.e., how to observe the Sabbath or under what circumstances does it constitute stealing, etc.). But more important, the Decalogue is a basic creed; it speaks of what one must do or refrain from doing in order to be counted as a member of this special community. As such, the complementary nature of the two sections is highly significant for they reflect the equal value of the two kinds of law. They also mirror two aspects of the covenant faith: love your God with all your heart and love your neighbor as yourself.

The Rabbis[1] of the Talmud also made two distinctions in the type of law: the one, between one human being and another; the other, between a human being and God. Yet, both types are laws between human beings and God. If one violates social ethics, it offends not only humanity and the social order; it is a sin against God. No matter that these cases are adjudicated in the courts of human enterprise; if you hurt your neighbor, then you violate the covenant with me, says God. The way you act with your fellow human being is determined by your relationship with me. (Deut. 15:7-10; 24:17-18; 25:13-16).

Thus, observance of the law becomes then a measure of integrity in the covenantal relationship. And always, always, the observance of law is linked to love.

> Therefore you shall love YHWH your God and keep his charge and his statutes and his ordinances and his commandments all the days. (Deut. 11:1)

To follow the commandments, ethical and moral as well as ritual and sacral, is felt not as an onerous duty but as an expression of love. There are still some who hold a stereotypic view of Judaism with regard to the salvific function of the law. This view maintains that love and law are dichotomous and that love is the fulfillment of law and can, therefore, replace it. However, a careful reading of Deuteronomy shows how inextricably linked are law and love. For a Jew to say, "I will" or "I do" is as powerful a statement of love as it is to say the words, "I love" or "I believe."

"Trivial" and Weighty Law

Love expresses itself in a thousand details, significant and trivial alike. So, too, is this great manifestation of covenant love concretized in statutes and commandments of differing degrees of gravity. The notion of importance and accessibility of all the law was embedded in the text in a variety of ways:

1. *Rabbi* spelled with a capital *R* refers always to the Rabbis of the Talmud. When this title is spelled with the lowercase *r* it refers to rabbis and scholars of all ages or of a particular time if so specified.

All the commandment which I command you this day, you shall observe
to do in order that you may live and multiply and go in and possess the
land which YHWH swore to your fathers. (Deut. 8:1)

Beware lest you forget YHWH your God in not keeping his commandments and statutes and ordinances which I command you this day. (Deut.
8:11)

In Deuteronomy can be found a number of these light commandments
in which there is more than meets the eye. Let us look at one example:

If you should happen to chance upon a bird's nest along your way, in
any tree or on the ground, with baby birds or eggs in it and the mother
sitting on the baby birds or the eggs, you shall not take the mother with
the offspring. You shall surely send away the mother and then you may
take the offspring, so that it goes well with you and you will prolong
your days. (Deut. 22:6-7)

The Rabbis cite this "bird nest" law as a classic case of a light
commandment (T.B. Hullin 142a). What makes it lightweight? The answer
is not given outright. Perhaps that it is a simple thing to do; just shoo the bird
away. Or perhaps it makes no difference. After all, birds don't remember their
children after sixty seconds. It seems almost trivial, especially when com-
pared with some of the grand ethical laws of Deuteronomy. What could there
possibly be in common between behavior regarding a bird's nest and the
prohibition against murder or adultery or false witness or treatment of slaves?
But the traditional commentators probe its inner meaning. Nachmanides,
a medieval exegete, comments that this law requires us to be compassionate
and kind to all sentient beings. A bird *does* suffer when a human being
approaches its nest of eggs or babies. Judaism teaches, from this law and from
others, that one must be ever alert not to be cruel to animal life. Be mindful of
a mother bird's cries not to cause her anguish, and this will surely train you to
be sensitive to the pain and anguish of all other living things.
A second lesson to draw from this light law, says Nachmanides, is
that of preservation of the species. If you take both the mother and the
offspring, you cut the line. If one is sensitive to this issue when it comes
to birds, who reproduce in great numbers and with great ease, then, a
fortiori, there will be sensitivity to continuity (perpetuity) of all species on
the ontological scale.

A third lesson, derived from these verses by the philosopher Maimonides, has to do with respect for parents. All parents feel pain at losing a child. It is not an intellectual matter but an emotional one; animals might feel it as much as humans. Thus it is no accident that the reward the Torah gives for honoring the feelings of a mother bird is the same as that of honoring one's parents — long life.

So important is this law, the Rabbis pointed out, that the Torah assigns it not one but two separate commandments: a prohibition — Thou shalt not take the mother with young — and a positive precept — Thou shalt surely send away the mother. So important was this law that the Rabbis established stringent guidelines: even if you have to send the mother bird away one hundred times (so that she will not be present when you take the young), take care to do so (T.B. Hullin 141b).

Covenant Renewal: What Happened to It?

Like all relationships of significance, the covenant must be continually renewed and reconsecrated. The book of Deuteronomy in itself is a symbol of that fact: barely one generation removed from the original covenant experience with all of its wondrous signs, there was a need to recovenant in the plains of Moab. Not only was the covenant reestablished anew there, but Moses, great leader that he was, set the pattern for future ceremonies. In every generation, in fact three or four times a generation, the people were to hear the Book of the Covenant being read. By their very presence, they would affirm their commitment to it (Deut. 31:9-13).

What happened to the covenant renewal ceremony? Unlike the covenant of Abraham, which is reenacted in the birth of every male child through the *brit* ("covenant") ceremony and is marked by a rite of circumcision, the covenant renewal of Sinai and Moab seems to have faded away over time. Many scholars believe that it disappeared after the Josianic reforms; others maintain that the ceremony was continued by the Dead Sea community and that its public celebration ended after the destruction of that sect. Certainly the formal ceremony is gone by the Rabbinic Age.

Yet, the covenant idea remained a powerful and central theme of Judaism, experienced alternately as a covenant with God and as the tight bond of a community — each Jew bound up with every other Jew in the covenant. How has the idea been carried forward to our day, making these words of Deuteronomy come alive:

Not only with you do I make this covenant but with him who stands
here this day before YHWH and also with him who is not here today.
(Deut. 29:13-14)

First and foremost is the centrality of the Torah, the Pentateuch. The
people of the Book and the people of the covenant are synonymous. The
traditional aphorism, "Israel, the Torah and the Holy Blessed One are one,"
sums up the covenantal relationship. Throughout Deuteronomy, the word
Torah is used interchangeably to mean the law, the law book, and the book
of the covenant.

The Torah, to this very day, is written in a special way by a scribe on a
parchment scroll. A consecutive portion of the scroll is read aloud in the
synagogue on each Sabbath morning and, in smaller segments, on Monday
and Thursday mornings, every week of the year. The Pentateuch is read in its
entirety once a year. On the day that the last chapter of Deuteronomy is
concluded, the first chapter of Genesis is begun anew. This holiday, called
Simchat Torah, "rejoicing of the Torah," was a creation of the rabbis of the
Middle Ages, one of the many attempts of leadership throughout the generations to keep Torah and covenant at the center of people's lives. Even those
liberal denominations that have adopted a triennial cycle of reading the
Pentateuch celebrate the continuous round of reading the Torah.

The Torah is regularly kept in an ark and is removed for the public
reading and returned with a certain ceremonial splendor. Words from
Deuteronomy are chanted by the congregation during this taking out and
putting back. Before the reading, this verse is recited by all: "And you
who cling to YHWH your God, all of you are alive today" — words
evoking the ancestors as they stood in the plains of Moab (Deut. 4:4).
Following the reading, the Torah is held aloft in two hands, scrolls held
apart as the carrier swivels around slowly in place so that all the congregation can see the writing and chant these words: "And this is the Torah
which Moses set before the children of Israel according to the word of
YHWH given into the hand of Moses" (Deut. 4:44). When certain pericopes
are read, such as the Decalogue, the entire congregation stands. When the
Deuteronomic blessings and curses are read, the former are read in a full
voice, the latter in barely a whisper.

At every important passage in life there is connection to the covenant.
At birth, it is the covenant of Abraham. At puberty, one's entry in Jewish
adulthood (age thirteen for males, twelve for females) is marked by vol-
untary acceptance of commandment, similar to the Jews of Sinai and Moab

who agreed to take upon themselves the yoke of commandments. Thus the terms *bar/bat-mitzvah,* "son/daughter of the commandments." At death the surviving family recites the Kaddish prayer, affirming even at that moment of grief the belief in one God.

The holiday of Pentecost was transformed over time from a primarily agricultural thanksgiving to one that celebrates the giving of the Torah. The portions describing the epiphany at Sinai and the giving of the Torah are read in the synagogue, with the entire congregation standing as if to receive the Torah anew. Take heed, says Deuteronomy 4:9-10, not to forget the things that you saw with your own eyes at Sinai, and tell it to your children and to their children. Many rituals of this holiday carry this covenant theme. Similarly, Passover, the holiday of the Exodus, imparts the message: each Jew is to feel as if he or she was taken personally out of Egypt and stood with the crowd at the foot of Sinai receiving, accepting the Torah there.

Yet, perhaps the most powerful, steadiest, and most frequent expression of the covenant idea comes in the daily liturgy. In special prayers, such as the psalm of the day reserved for Thursday mornings, one discovers a replica of the covenant formulary and its Deuteronomic themes. Above all, the organization of the *Shma* prayer by the Rabbis (Deut. 6:4-9; 11:13-21; also Num. 15:37-41) and the significance they attached to it has the most profound covenantal implications.

The *Shma* has always been known as the central creed of the Jewish faith. It is the centerpiece of the morning and evening prayers. It is recited by a Jew upon retiring for the night. Its opening verses are the first prayer a Jewish child is taught. When death approaches, the *Shma* is to be the last words on one's lips. Of all the prayers in the Jewish liturgy, this is the one for which there is an absolute requirement of *kavannah* — conscious, intentional devotion. Thoughts may wander in formal prayer, acknowledged the Rabbis, but when it comes to the *Shma,* set your mind on it before you proceed. Don't run it into other prayers but set it apart. Recite it in any language that you understand. Listen to your own words as you recite them. These are but some of the rabbinic parameters for praying this prayer (see B.T. Berachot 13a-16b).

Jon Levenson says that the *Shma* contains all the elements of the covenant formulary:[2] the classic statement of covenant monotheism — "Hear, O Israel, the Lord our God, the Lord is One"; the central stipulation

---

2. On the theme of covenant and the *Shma* prayer, see Jon Levenson, *Sinai and Zion* (New York: Harper and Row, 1983).

to love God expressed in carrying out the commandments; the dangers of seduction; the curses and the blessings; the witness of natural phenomenon, heaven and earth. Even the covenant formulary criterion to deposit the text and periodically reread it can be found in the *Shma:* the requirement constantly to recite "these words" and to write them on the door posts of one's house and to symbolize them on one's clothing are the equivalents.

Why is the word *covenant* or *renewal ceremony* not mentioned? This is wholly consistent with the rabbinic pattern of making the everyday holy, and the sacred, routine. Just as they moved the sacrificial cult from an occasional dramatic offering into the home with continuous blessings, worship, and service of the heart, so they moved what was an extraordinary covenantal ceremony into daily life where consciousness of the covenant relationship could become deeply and permanently embedded in the soul and psyche of every Jew.

The covenant with Abraham formed the Jewish people. The covenant at Sinai defined and shaped them. The covenant in the plains of Moab reinforced and expanded the relationship; the record of that event in Deuteronomy contributed significantly to perpetuating the covenant faith and experience.

Contributors

ELIZABETH ACHTEMEIER Adjunct Professor of Bible and Homiletics at Union Theological Seminary in Virginia since 1973. Lecturer and author of numerous articles and books, including *Preaching from the Old Testament.* Her latest book, *Nature, God, and Pulpit,* published by Eerdmans, appeared in 1992.

JOSEPH CARDINAL BERNADIN Archbishop of Chicago since 1982. Member of many committees, including the Pontifical Commission for the Revision of Canon Law. Author of numerous statements on a variety of subjects (e.g., concerning the education of children, the priesthood, the AIDS crisis) and leader in interfaith dialogue. Recipient of the Albert Einstein International Peace Prize, 1983.

LAWRENCE BOADT Professor of Biblical Studies at the Washington Theological Union in Silver Spring, Maryland. His special fields of interest are the Ancient Near Eastern background to the Bible and the Prophets, but he has written books and articles covering a wide range of biblical topics. His most recent volume is *Reading the Old Testament: An Introduction,* 1984.

WALTER BRUEGGEMANN Professor of Old Testament at Columbia Theological Seminary, Decatur, Georgia. Past President of the Society of Biblical Literature, lecturer, author of numerous articles and books. His most recent volumes include the two published by Eerdmans: *Jeremiah 26–52: To Build and Plant* (1988) and *Jeremiah 26–52: To Build and Plant* (1991).

A. STANLEY DREYFUS Since 1967, part-time Lecturer at the New York School of Hebrew Union College–Jewish Institute of Religion. During his tenure as Chairperson of the Liturgy Committee of the Central Conference of American

Rabbis, several volumes have appeared for the use of Reform Congregations, including the well-known, *Gates of Prayer* (1975).

KATHLEEN FARMER Professor of Old Testament at United Theological Seminary in Dayton, Ohio, since 1978. Contributor of articles and chapters in journals and books as well as author of several books, including, *Proverbs and Ecclesiastes: Who Knows What Is Good?* (Eerdmans, 1991). Forthcoming is her commentary on the book of Ruth for the *New Interpreter's Bible* commentary.

DONALD E. GOWAN Professor of Old Testament at Pittsburgh Theological Seminary since 1965 and coeditor of *Horizons in Biblical Theology.* Among the many articles and books that he has written are: *Eschatology in the Old Testament* and *Genesis 1–11: From Eden to Babel* (Eerdmans, 1988).

BLU GREENBERG Blu Greenberg writes and lectures extensively on subjects of Jewish scholarly and contemporary interest. She is the author of *On Women and Judaism, How to Run a Traditional Jewish Household, A Special Kind of Mother and Other Poems* and has published numerous articles.

FREDRICK C. HOLMGREN Professor of Biblical Literature at North Park Theological Seminary in Chicago since 1960. Coeditor of the multi-volume *International Theological Commentary* (Eerdmans) and author of articles and several books on Old Testament texts. The most recent volume is: *Ezra-Nehemiah: Israel Alive Again* (Eerdmans, 1987).

SAMUEL KARFF Senior Rabbi of Congregation Beth Israel, Houston, Texas, and Lecturer in the Department of Religious Studies at Rice University. Among Rabbi Karff's publications is *Agada: The Language of Jewish Faith.* Rabbi Karff has served on many important committees and is a former President of the Central Conference of Jewish Rabbis.

JEROME R. MALINO A former President of the Central Conference of American Rabbis and Adjunct Lecturer in Homiletics at the Hebrew Union College–Jewish Institute of Religion. Dr. Malino has served as President of the Institute on Religion in the Age of Science, contributed to professional journals, and published original and translated poetry.

GUNTHER PLAUT Rabbi and Senior Scholar at Holy Blossom Temple, Toronto, Canada. Dr. Plaut has authored numerous articles and books on theology, history, and philosophy. His most recent volume, of which he is both editor and chief author, is: *The Torah: A Modern Commentary* (7th ed., 1991).

HERMAN SCHAALMAN Rabbi at Emanuel Congregation of Chicago since 1955. Dr. Schaalman holds the Jewish Chautaugua Society resident lectureship at Garrett Evangelical Seminary and Chicago Theological Seminary and is a former President of the Central Conference of American Rabbis. In 1986 Jewish and Christian colleagues published a volume of essays in his honor: *The Life of Covenant: The Challenge of Contemporary Judaism* (ed. J. A. Edelheit).

LOU H. SILBERMAN Professor Silberman has held faculty appointments at Vanderbilt University. As a Visiting Professor, he has also taught at other universities, including University of Vienna, University of Chicago, and Duke University. Prof. Silberman served on the editorial boards of major journals and is a former President of the Society of Biblical Literature.

†**CARROLL STUHLMUELLER** Dr. Stuhlmueller served for twenty-five years as Professor of Old Testament Studies at Catholic Theological Union, Chicago, Illinois. In addition to his many books and articles on biblical themes, he has written on a number of contemporary issues, for example, peace, the poor as well as women and the priesthood. His most recent volumes are: *Rebuilding with Hope: Haggai and Zechariah* (Eerdmans, 1987) and *New Paths through the Old Testament* (1989).

DAVID TRACY Internationally known theologian and author who is Professor of Theology and Catholic Studies at the Divinity School of the University of Chicago. Invited Lecturer and Visiting Professor at major universities and author of many books and articles, including his well-known *The Analogical Imagination: Christian Theology and the Culture of Pluralism,* 1981. His most recent volume is: *Dialogue with the Other: The Interreligious Dialogue* (Eerdmans, 1991).

ELIE WIESEL Noted Jewish scholar, novelist, and lecturer who broke the silence of the Jewish and Christian communities after World War II and began to speak about the unspeakable, the Holocaust — the murder of six million Jews. His first book spoke out of his own experiences in the concentration camps and appeared in French in 1958 (*La Nuit*) and in English (*Night*) in 1969. Some twenty or more books followed. Recently there appeared *Sages and Dreamers: Biblical, Talmudic and Hasidic Portraits and Legends,* 1991.

Index of Scripture References

I. OLD TESTAMENT

II. NEW TESTAMENT

III. APOCRYPHA AND PSEUDEPIGRAPHA

Testament of Dan
5:3   126

Testament of Issachar
5:2   126

Tobit
4:15   127

IV. BABYLONIAN TALMUD

Aboth
2:15   127

4:15   127

Sabbat
31a   127

V. RABBINIC LITERATURE

Genesis Rabba
38:1-10   19n
40:8   130n

Exodus Rabba
2:2   65

2:4   63
2:5   62, 70, 71
2:6   63, 72
32:1   91-92
43:2   91-92

Leviticus Rabba
12:1   106
12:3   106
20:10   111n